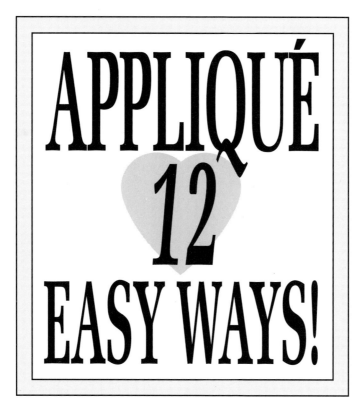

APPLIQUÉ 12 EASY WAYS!

Charming Quilts, Giftable Projects, and Timeless Techniques

by Elly Sienkiewicz

C&T PUBLISHING

Aleene's Hot Stitch Fusible Web is a trademark of
    Aleene's Division, Artis, Inc.
Bernina #1230 is a registered trademark of
    Fritz Gegauf, Ltd.
Bias Press Bars is a product of Pat Andreatta.
Celtic Bias Bars is a trademark of Philomena Wiechek.
Classic Metal Iron is a trademark of the Black & Decker
    Corporation.
Dritz Fray Check is a trademark of the Sewing Notions
    Division of Risdon Corporation.
Magic Sizing is a registered trademark of the Dial
    Corporation.
Morning Glory Batting is a registered trademark of the
    Taylor Bedding Manufacturing Company.
Mylar is a registered trademark of E. I. duPont de
    Nemours & Co.
Pigma Micron is a registered trademark of the Sakura
    Color Products Corporation of America.
Pilot SC-UF Extra Fine Point Permanent Marker is a
    product of the Pilot Corporation of America.
Reynold's Freezer Paper is a registered trademark of the
    Consumer Products Division, Reynold's Metal
    Company.
Scotch and Spray Mount Artist's Adhesive are registered
    trademarks of the 3M Corporation.
Spray Adhesive for Art, Crafts, and Hobby is a trademark
    of M. Grumbacher Company, Inc.
Sticky Stuff is a registered trademark of the Clotilde
    Company.
Wonder-Under is a registered trademark of the Pellon
    Division, Freudenberg Nonwovens.
Baltimore Beauties is a registered trademark of
    Elly Sienkiewicz.

Photographs by Sharon Risedorph, San Francisco,
    unless otherwise noted.
Edited by Sayre Van Young, Berkeley, California.
Technical information edited by Janet Macik Myers,
    Fairfield, California.
Book design, illustration, and production by
    Julie Olson Design and Illustration, Washington, D.C.

Copyright © 1991 Eleanor Patton Hamilton Sienkiewicz

Published by C&T Publishing, Inc.
P.O. Box 1456
Lafayette, CA 94549

ISBN: 0-914881-42-6

Sienkiewicz, Elly.
    Appliqué 12 easy ways : charming quilts, giftable projects,
and timeless techniques / by Elly Sienkiewicz.
        p.   cm.
    Includes bibliographical references.
    ISBN 0-914881-42-6 : $14.95
        1. Appliqué. 2. Appliqué–Patterns. I. Title. II. Title:
Appliqué twelve easy ways.
TT779.S53 1991
746.44'5—dc20

Library of Congress Card No: 91-53029
First Edition

Printed in Hong Kong

10   9   8

*Front Cover Photo: Detail of "You've Stolen My Heart!"
(Project #1). This was the author's earliest appliqué learning
sampler. The quilting is by Joyce Hill. A similar quilt, "Be My
Valentine" (Project #2), designed, appliquéd, and quilted by
Libby Hamilton Samuel, shows the same hearts, but sewn
with fine precision.*

Contents

Color Section follows page 40.

Acknowledgments

To all those quiltmakers who have considered heirloom appliqué "too hard" to try, thank you for your forthrightness. You'll find the projects in this book as easy to make as they are appealing. When you've completed just the hearts in Chapter 2, you'll know in your own heart that you can now appliqué just about anything.

To my publishers who saw a need for an appliqué technique and project book, thank you for inviting me to join you in this. And thank you, from me as a quilter as well as an author, for putting so much pride and concomitant resources into your fine books for us all.

To each generous needleartist whose considerable quiltmaking skills and honorably kept commitments created projects for this book, thank you for all. I'm also most grateful to those individuals and institutions whose open sharing of their work and photographs helped make this book possible.

Thank you for the inspiration, to fellow author Joen Wolfrom and to Mary Sharp, vice-president in charge of marketing, Morning Glory Batting Division of the Taylor Bedding Manufacturing Company, who urged that I "do something simple for appliqué." Morning Glory Batting's generous contribution of batting and pillow forms for projects in this book is also gratefully acknowledged. To this book's production team—Diane Pedersen, tireless C & T editor and production manager; Sayre Van Young, my editor for the fourth book in a row (for which I am grateful); Janet Macik Myers, pattern editor; and Julie Olson, talented illustrator and now book designer—thank you for bringing this book to life.

My special thanks to our friend and noted calligrapher Walter J. Filling whose calligraphy has been traced onto the keepsake quilt, "Katya's Album"; to my cousin Libby Hamilton Samuel for accepting the design commission to make the charming quilt, "Be My Valentine"; to my assistant Denise Scott for substantial and competent support graciously given; to Carol Elliott, Audrey Waite, and Mary Sue Hannan for fine assembly and machine work on several of my pieces; to Peggy Frangos for pattern checking; and to both Tom and Mary Sue Hannan for friendship and a helping hand.

And thank you dear family, Donald, Alex, Katya, and Stan (who, along with all else, patiently helped me with the math). Alex, you said, "You were never a milk-and-cookies kind of mom." Well, I really was once, for a little while, back before you can remember. And I'd like to be again. But meanwhile, thanks for all the help—and the homemade cookies!

♡♡♡

Dedication

This book, written during the Gulf War crisis, is dedicated to our son, Pfc. Donald Hamilton Sienkiewicz, my Marine. Among those who "also serve who only sit and wait," he during this time earned academic stars in the NROTC at Boston University. To Donald, and to all of our police and armed forces who risk their lives that law and order rule in a world where real evil still exists, thank you for letting the quiltmaking continue.

How to Use This Book

Tradition. Tradition is at the heart of quiltmaking. It calls to us all. And always there, from quilt-making's traditional beginnings, has been appliqué. Appliqué, the applying of fabric decoration to a larger surface, is a stream in our quilt heritage whose time has come round again. Delightfully versatile, she is in full bloom in interior decorations, on clothing, and on quilts. It seems as though everyone either wants to learn how to appliqué or is already doing it. Lucky for us, so many have shared their insights that modern ingenuity combines with appliqué tradition to teach us all we need to know. For almost two decades, I've been teaching quilt-making professionally. Unquestionably, one of my most popular appliqué classes has been "You've Stolen My Heart: Twelve Ways to Appliqué." Twelve ways and still counting, for appliqué seems to be an ongoing process of learning and developing finer and more effective techniques. My goal in this book is to teach hand appliqué through the easy format of that heart quilt class. The second chapter does just that.

After the basic lessons, we'll move on to three more specialized methods (especially useful for fruits and flowers) in Chapter 3. You'll learn these techniques on a delightful pillow, "Dutch Bulbs a-Bloomin'." Chapter 4 has fabric specifications and assembly instructions for giftable projects, then small quilts, and finally bed quilts, those practical heirlooms of tomorrow. For each design, yardage and cutting requirements are given. Simple assembly instructions are combined with a master drawing of the project and its patterns. Projects are ranked for ease of making, with appropriate methods listed from Chapters 2 and 3. Always check back to see what supplies are needed and to remind yourself how the method is done. Be sure to look at the color photos too, as they suggest possible color combinations.

To ground our approach firmly in this modern era (and because our models are made by both hand and machine), I've included my personal hints for machine appliqué, or (to borrow a phrase from author Harriet Hargrave), "hand sewing with an electric needle." With no pretense at writing definitively about that now frontier-breaking field, I'd like to share those methods for machine appliqué that have helped me. With quilts and decorations made relatively quickly, mechanization encourages the making of modern traditions. Many of these machine-aided projects will be used up in daily living, but they will have enriched the lives of those we love. The memory of them will keep alive this deep and abiding affection we all have for quilts.

Above all, *Appliqué 12 Easy Ways!* will give you a solid foundation in hand appliqué. It shows hand appliqué's versatility and inspires with a delightful variety of patterned projects, large and small. Our detailed instructions focus on the appliqué process itself, rather than on construction of the completed project. Brief assembly notes are included. Finishing the projects involves simple, straightforward sewing. If assembly and finishing are a problem, advice from your sewing shop or a book on the subject from the public library should help. For the basics of quiltmaking, the classic *How to Make a Quilt* by Bonnie Leman covers it all (available from Quilts and Other Comforts, Quilter's Newsletter Magazine, P. O. Box 394-APP, Wheatridge, CO 80034-0394).

PATTERN TRANSFER: There are four basic ways to transfer an appliqué pattern. You can transfer a pattern by:

1. Drawing around a cut-out template. Note that all patterns in this book are finished size. Draw around them and add the seam allowance to that shape.
2. Tracing the pattern onto the rough side of freezer paper, cutting it out, and ironing it (shiny side down) onto the right side of the fabric. You can then draw around the pattern and remove it. Or, for Method #2 or #4, leave the paper pattern on to make the appliqué easier. When a part of an appliqué pattern is shown—half, a quarter, or an eighth—tracing it onto a folded sheet of freezer paper (the size of the finished unit) and then cutting all the layers at once will give you the complete pattern.
3. Using dressmaker's carbon paper and following the directions on the package to trace the pattern to the right side of the appliqué cloth.
4. Using a lightbox to trace the pattern directly to the right side of the appliqué cloth.

CHAPTER 1

Introducing Appliqué

Appliqué is the sewing of decorative cloth shapes onto background material. We call these top pieces the "appliqués," the ones applied to the foundation. There's a delightful freedom in the variety of shapes to be sewn to the base fabric. And there are different ways to sew the appliqué to its base. You are about to learn twelve of the best methods. Nine of these use unobtrusive (nondecorative) stitches and a turned-under seam. The tenth, the blanket stitch, is a decorative stitch over a raw edge. The last two methods deal with stem-like lines and grape-like circles. There's even a baker's dozen thirteenth way: dimensional appliqué.

Learning the Stitches

There are two basic, nondecorative stitches for hand appliqué: the tack stitch and the blind stitch. Each has multiple versions, any one of which will do for getting started. Whichever stitch you use most will become the best way for you—and you may even come up with a unique stitch style of your own. Note that in describing the path of the thread for various stitches, I'll use this book's front cover as a model. The appliqué fabric will be the "red" and the background, the "blue."

Left-handers, the instructions and supporting illustrations are for right-handed sewing; you will need to reverse them.

THE TACK STITCH

Tack stitches are like staples. They come up through the appliqué and go into the background. There are two versions: the first—what I call the "tack stitch out the fold"—is the least visible; the second—the "tack stitch catching the fold"—is slightly more visible but quicker and possibly stronger. It's the stitch I currently use the most.

THE TACK STITCH OUT THE FOLD

The needle comes up through the blue background and out through the fold of the red appliqué. Then it re-enters the blue background just under the edge of the fold, directly opposite where it came out of the fold (Figure 1-1 A). Tuck the needle under the edge of the red so that its point

aims toward the hole where it came out of the background (Figure 1-1 B). Next scrape your underneath finger with the needle, swing it away from you, and bring it up through the blue and out the fold of the red again (Figure 1-1 C). You go back into the blue fabric straight under where you came out the red fold, tugging the thread slightly so that the tiniest possible amount of it shows.

FIGURE 1-1 A–C.
The tack stitch out the fold.

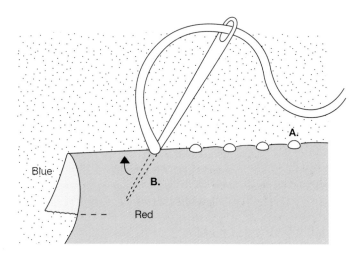

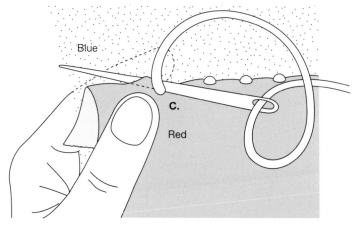

FIGURE 1-2 A-D.
The tack stitch catching the fold.

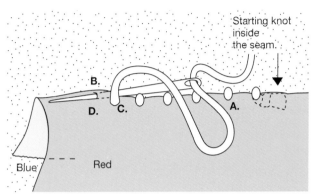

FIGURE 1-3 C-D.
The ladder stitch.

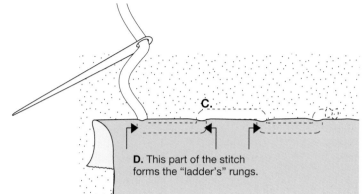

None of the forward motion of the thread is on top of the fabric; it's all underneath. You'll see the dashed line of your stitches moving forward on the back.

THE TACK STITCH CATCHING THE FOLD
Leaving more thread showing, this stitch takes a tiny bite out of the fold (Figure 1-2 A). When you bring the needle up through the blue background, come through the red appliqué so that one side of the needle's shank touches the fold (Figure 1-2 B). Pull the needle through and take it over the edge, back into the hole it came out (Figure 1-2 C). It will leave a thread bite at the edge of the fold that is just the width of the needle's shank. Because you are moving parallel to your body, you can just catch the fold rather than swinging the needle away from you to come out the fold. Thus this stitch is a quicker motion than the tack stitch out the fold. It seems stronger as well, because even with the narrowest seams, the needle always tacks two layers of fabric (the top appliqué and its turned-under seam) to the background (Figure 1-2 D).

THE BLIND STITCH AND ITS VARIANTS
The blind stitch and its variants follow a quite different thread path. Take a stitch into and out of the blue background, then directly opposite where the needle comes

out, enter the red appliqué's fold, take a stitch, and exit the fold (Figure 1-3 A). The needle takes, repeatedly, a stitch into and out of the background, then a stitch into and out of the fold (Figure 1-3 B). The path the thread thus follows gives it the name the ladder stitch (Figure 1-3 C). And like a ladder, the rungs have to be both horizontal and parallel (Figure 1-3 D). If they move forward on the diagonal, the stitches will be loose and visible and awfully hard to climb! If they enter into the blue directly opposite where they come out the "tunnel" of the red (and enter the red directly opposite where they come out of the blue), they will not only be climbable, they won't show.

FIGURE 1-3 E-F.
The slip stitch and the running stitch.

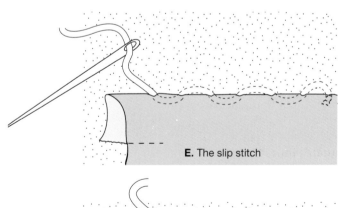

FIGURE 1-3 A-B.
The blind stitch.

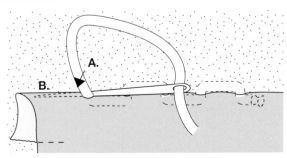

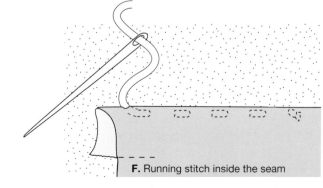

If, instead of taking this stitch in two steps (a stitch into and out of the fold, a stitch into and out of the background), you run them together, three or so at a time, then tug the thread, you'll slip the stitches to completion. This slip stitch is invisible, and because you take several stitches for one pull of the thread, it is also speedy (Figure 1-3 E). When you condense this stitch, it's as though you are taking a running stitch through the turned-under seam (right at the fold) and the background (Figure 1-3 F). This running stitch inside the seam is very fast, indeed. By any name, the blind stitch is useful wherever there are nice expanses of straightforward appliqué. For points or corners or tiny tight curves, go back to the tack stitch.

THREAD BEGINNINGS AND ENDINGS

If you begin your sewing by entering underneath the blue, the knot will sit on the back of your piece (Figure 1-4). To hide your knot, begin the first stitch by slipping the needle inside the folded-under seam of the red. When you pull the thread through, the knot will come to rest inside the seam. You want to finish off your thread neatly and not leave a tail that, under a thin white background fabric, might show. To end, take three tight stitches on top of each other on the back, under the cover of an appliqué. Or tie a French knot (a "tailor's knot") over the last stitch on the back. To tie a French knot (Figure 1-4 A), stop sewing when you still have 5"-6" of thread left. Slip the needle under the last stitch taken on the back of your work. Take the end of the thread coming from the fabric and wind it around the neck of the needle two times. Pinch these wound threads (between thumb and forefinger) against the background fabric to hold them in place while you pull the needle on through.

Finishing Touches: Pressing and Quilting Appliqué

Some people never press their appliqué. I always do. But it needs to be done with the top appliqué side down onto a layer of terry towel. A press cloth on the back helps to avoid catching stitches. Steam ironing or using a bit of spray starch from the back seems to press the appliqué to a neat and tidy finished look. As far as quilting appliqué goes, you can either quilt up to the shapes, or you can actually quilt through the shapes. In general, the style seems to be to quilt up to small-scale appliqués (under 3½" or so), but not through them. You can "echo quilt" around them. Echo the appliqué stitches in repeated rows, like ripples radiating from a pebble tossed in a pond. Or you can outline quilt (right next to the appliqué, or just ¼" beyond it) and use filler quilting patterns (parallel diagonal lines, diamond grids, clamshells, etc.) in between the shapes. In some cases, you may want to quilt the central vein of a leaf for both sturdiness and artistry, or you may want to quilt a design into a larger appliqué.

FIGURE 1-4 A-B.
French knot finish.

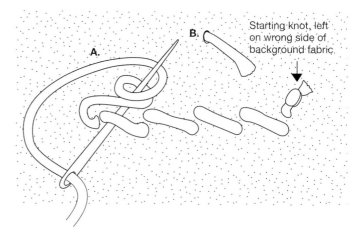

Starting knot, left on wrong side of background fabric.

After tying the knot, thread the needle between the fabric layers and bring it up about an inch away through the background fabric. Clip the thread, and tug the cloth so the thread tail disappears back under the appliqué.

Today, many quilters have started trimming back the background fabric underneath the appliqué to within ¼" of the seam, so the quilting will be easier (through one layer only) and will puff nicely. I have never seen a nineteenth-century quilt in which the background was cut out from behind an appliqué. To do so gives the appliqué itself a flat look, like patchwork. In the end, it seems simply a matter of taste. What do I do? On large-scale machine appliqué (particularly ones of 5" or more), I cut out the back; on hand appliqué, I leave it intact.

Basic Equipment for Appliqué

PINS: You'll need small safety pins for major basting in Method #1 or #2, and short fine straight pins (called pleater or sequin pins) for use in any methods where you wish to pin, rather than baste, the shapes to the background cloth.

NEEDLES: A long thin needle is ideal for hand appliqué. The length helps you turn under curves and points. As with all needles, the size of the needle's diameter goes down as the number size of the needle goes up. Especially good for appliqué are Sharps #11 and Milliner's Needles #11.

THREAD: Machine-weight thread works for hand appliqué. You can buy both mercerized cotton-covered polyester thread and 100% cotton thread appropriate for appliqué. There's a lot of stretch to synthetic fibers—take 12 inches of 100% polyester thread and pull it. It will give and shrink back a bit, as a piece of elastic would. To avoid "shrinking" your appliqué, stay away from 100% polyester thread, or "lingerie thread" with substantial amounts of nylon in it, or 100% nylon thread. I prefer 100% cotton and 100% silk thread; these less stretchy natural fiber threads are excellent for more controlled hand appliqué. The higher the weight number, the finer, more easily hidden, the thread. I use 50 to 60 weight 100% cotton machine embroidery threads.

THREAD COLOR: Up until this century, appliqué was usually done in white or very pale thread. Most appliquérs now match their thread color to the color of the top appliqué fabric. If you have no close match, or the colors in the piece of cloth vary wildly, try to match the shade in gray or beige. Using the least visible stitch, the blind stitch, also helps hide the thread.

MONOFILAMENT: Very fine clear or smoke-colored transparent 100% nylon thread (monofilament) is used by many for blind hemstitching on the sewing machine as well as for machine quilting. It can also be used for fine hand sewing. I find it relaxing to use when a fine-scale piece would have to be sewn in a wide variety of colors.

The transparent thread means you can sew right along without having to change thread color repeatedly. And hiding the stitches is a cinch with it! Remember not to pull this thread too tight, not to iron it too hot, and not to iron without a press cloth. Some find the idea of fine hand sewing with such modern thread heresy. (I resisted it for several years.) Further, they worry that over time, the rugged synthetic thread may cut that softer natural fiber cloth. For my part, I heed Ellen Peter's recommendation of this thread; when it suits my mood and needs, I use it.

SCISSORS: Small, sharp, cut-to-the-point scissors are needed for hand appliqué. The 5" "tailor-point" scissors are ideal. If your scissors are too big or do not cut to the point, you will undercut inward points, or double-cut them, or over-cut them. All of these lead to fray and inaccuracy. To test whether your scissors cut to the point, place their tips across a corner, exactly at the edge of the paper; they should cut the corner off cleanly. If they do not cut to the point, get them serviced (or get new ones) so that you can cut inward points accurately.

AIDS TO VISION AND TO COMFORT: You need to see better for appliqué than for reading the phone book, for example. Use a magnifier around your neck, or a magnifying light, or magnifying glasses as needed. Good light directly on the work helps. Eyes are like muscles, so you see better in the morning when they are refreshed by sleep. Keep your appliqué at the best distance for seeing well. This may mean working at a table, or sewing with a pillow in your lap to rest your hands on as you work.

SPRAY STARCH: Spray starch is needed for Method #9. Spray sizing is also useful for putting a bit of body back into pre-washed fabric, or for holding a turned seam under more strongly. In addition, Magic® Sizing inhibits bleeding in the Pilot® SC-UF pen, used to write on quilts. For caution's sake, spray and iron the wrong side of the fabric unless directions indicate otherwise.

DRESSMAKER'S CARBON: Dressmaker's carbon paper or dressmaker's transfer paper work just like regular typing carbon paper. Place the pattern on the top, then the transfer paper, waxy side down to the right side of the fabric. Graphite pattern transfer paper works in the same fashion and is sold at craft stores or woodworking shops. Avoid papers whose marks will "disappear" after a few hours. And never iron carbon paper tracings—that can make them permanent. Wash tracings out thoroughly first, if the piece is to be ironed. I like to draw over the original pattern's lines with a blue ballpoint pen, pressing hard to transfer them through the carbon paper. The drawn blue line on my pattern shows me what I've already traced.

MARKING PENS AND PENCILS: A fine mechanical pencil can be used for marking light-colored fabrics. Numerous light-colored pencils are available to mark dark fabrics. They can be bought at fabric or quilt shops. Better-quality colored pencils for artwork also work well: try silver, yellow, white, pink, or light blue. There are several "washout" felt-tipped pens made for fabric, but I avoid them for hand appliqué. They draw a rather thick line and the blue can mysteriously return. For the ease of a pen, I prefer to use the acid-free permanent Pigma Micron® pen with the letters SDK marked on the side (signifying it's a permanent pen). It comes in many sizes; use the finest (.005 or .01) to mark an easily turned-under appliqué seam line. This pen comes in a variety of colors; the brown is particularly unobtrusive and marks many fabric shades well. The Pigma Micron is one of the two pens I prefer for drawing and writing on fabric. The other is the Pilot SC-UF pen in black; it's a bit heavy for marking an appliqué turn line, but it's excellent for inscribing projects.

LIGHTBOX: When you use a lightbox to transfer a pattern, the pattern goes on the bottom (illustration facing up) and whatever cloth you are tracing onto goes over the top of it. You can trace directly onto the appliqué fabric using a fine Pigma Micron pen (or other marker) to mark the turn line. Use a lightbox to trace onto template material (plastic or file folders), or to help position appliqués on the background fabric.

TEMPLATE MATERIALS: Templates are pattern shapes to draw around to transfer the design to cloth. They are an easy way to transfer simple appliqué patterns like the heart in Chapter 2. Templates can be made of transparent or translucent plastic such as sheets of Mylar®, or translucent plastic cut from plastic jugs or other packaging. The advantage of plastic is that you can see through it to trace a shape. Its cut edges also hold up longer than paper after repeated tracings. Plastic can sometimes be marked in lead pencil. If not, use one of the permanent pens already mentioned. Lightweight cardboard (file cards, manila folders, cereal boxes, cardboard from stocking packages) makes excellent templates. White poster board makes a substantial template ideal for use with spray starch. High-tech templates can be made with adhesive papers: sheets of label paper, color-coding office dots, and self-sticking shelf papers.

FREEZER PAPER AS A TEMPLATE MATERIAL: Freezer paper (Reynold's® Freezer Paper, the supermarket brand, or butchers' freezer paper) has wonderful properties as appliqué template material. It is inexpensive, comes in long sheets, is easy to draw on, is transparent enough to use as tracing paper, and is light enough to staple (to keep the layers from shifting) and to stack cut. Its shiny side is poly-coated and adheres to fabric when ironed. You need a hot (cotton setting), dry iron and a hard board (like a bread board) to iron on. Always do a test piece first. For freezer paper appliqué, 100% cotton works best. If the paper lifts up too easily and gets in the way, the solution is a hot iron, a hard board, and a heavy hand. For a freezer-paper-on-the-top method (Methods #2 and #4), you need a very hot, rather heavy iron. Older irons which get scorching hot are ideal. The only modern iron I know of which gets hot enough is the Classic™, an all-steel-bottomed iron by Black & Decker. Try to compensate for the low-regulated heat of other modern irons by preheating them and pressing very very hard, particularly at points. For freezer paper used inside (Method #8), a nonscorching iron works well because you really don't want the freezer paper to adhere so tightly that it tugs at the raw seam edges when you pull it out.

SEWING MACHINE: When sewing machines first came into use, appliqué with the straight stitch over a turned-under edge showed one's new skills. If done that way today, transparent nylon thread is frequently used. More often now, the zigzag or satin stitch (in matching thread) is used over a raw edge. Increasingly though, sewers are using the blind hemstitch (and monofilament) for unobtrusive machine appliqué over a turned-under edge. The patterns in this book could be done on the sewing machine as well as by hand.

FABRIC: Traditionally, calico-weight cotton fabric (100% cotton, or 60% cotton/40% polyester) has been used for quilt appliqués. Cotton is easiest for appliqué because it holds a crease well and ages gracefully. By the time you have tried making hearts by all the methods in Chapter 2, you will have more control over the fabric for perfect points, curves, and inward corners. Along with this skill comes the ability to use a wider variety of fabrics. You'll find what you can and can't handle well. If the main issue is wear and washability, keep the fiber content consistent throughout a given project. Prewashing the fabric reassures you about the project's future washability. Prewash it as you would the finished product.

CHAPTER 2

You've Stolen My Heart: Ten Ways to Appliqué

V alentine's Day was in the offing and a wealth of red hearts on blue backgrounds sounded like fun. Project #1 was the result. One square has a reverse appliquéd ("missing") heart on which is written "You've Stolen My Heart!" Playing on the heart theme, Libby Samuel added small folk and called her quilt "Be My Valentine" (Project #2). Both quilts invite you to play with color, cloth, and appliqué. Each project has varied blue backgrounds topped by assorted red heart fabrics. Throughout this chapter, I'll refer to the hearts as "red" and the background blocks as "blue." Of course, you can use any color combinations you like.

Skim the methods in this chapter. They teach ten ways to appliqué, one at a time, while you make one heart with each method. After you've finished the first ten hearts, you'll be basking in success and set to keep sewing. The next chapter introduces more complex appliqué, with a touch of layered floral appliqué and a simple folded ribbon flower (dimensional appliqué).

When you look over the projects in this book, specific methods for making each project are given. In each case, the first method listed will be the one I would choose. Some close second choices follow, then in parentheses, other applicable methods. I'll rate each project as we go, just for the ease of its appliqué. (Time being a totally separate issue!) Rankings are Super Easy!, Easy, Moderately Easy, and A Challenge. By the end of Chapter 3, you will have learned a baker's dozen ways to appliqué, and you'll surely be ready for the delights of all the projects to follow.

PROJECT #1
Small quilt: "You've Stolen My Heart!"
25" x 30".
Designed by Elly Hamilton Sienkiewicz.

PROJECT #2
Small quilt: "Be My Valentine."
25" x 30".
Designed by Libby Hamilton Samuel.

Suggested Methods: Use all ten ways to appliqué, since these little quilts are learning samplers.

Appliqué Ease Level: Because there's so much to learn in this chapter, it seems a bit unfeeling to call Project #1's pattern "Super Easy!" But if I were to rank it based on doing it by the very easiest method, it would be just that. Project #2, with its people and reverse appliqué border, is rated "Moderately Easy."

Fabric for Project #1
- *Blue background fabric (templates B, D, and Q,):* assorted scraps or ⅜ yard blue. To get fabric prepared for assorted methods, cut 28 squares 4" x 4".
- *Red fabric for hearts (templates A and C):* assorted scraps or ⅜ yard. To get fabric prepared for 28 hearts for assorted methods, cut 28 squares 4" x 4".
- *White for the missing heart:* small 4" x 4" scrap
- *White fabric for border E and F:* ¼ yard. To get a top and bottom border, each ½" x 10", finished, cut 2 rectangles 1" x 10½". To get two side borders, each ½" x 15", finished, cut two rectangles 1" x 15½".
- *Blue fabric for border G and H:* ¼ yard. To get a top and bottom border, each 1½" x 10", finished, cut two rectangles 2" x 10½". To get two side borders 1½" x 15", finished, cut two rectangles 2" x 15½".
- *Dark blue print for border I and J:* ¼ yard. To get a top and bottom border, each 2½" x 14", finished, cut two rectangles 3" x 14½". To get two side borders 2½" x 19", finished, cut two rectangles 3" x 19½".

PROJECT #1
Small quilt: "You've Stolen My Heart!"

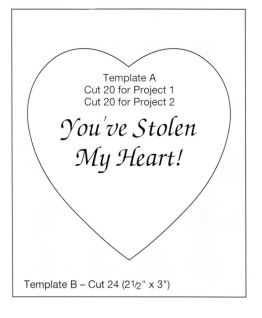

Template A
Cut 20 for Project 1
Cut 20 for Project 2

You've Stolen My Heart!

Template B – Cut 24 (2½" x 3")

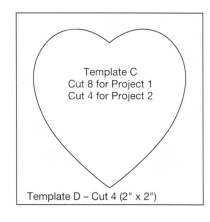

Template C
Cut 8 for Project 1
Cut 4 for Project 2

Template D – Cut 4 (2" x 2")

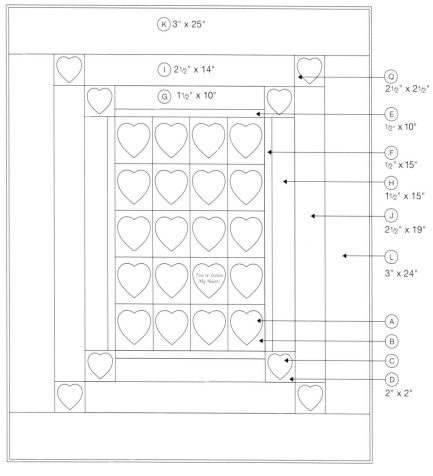

K 3" x 25"

I 2½" x 14"

G 1½" x 10"

Q 2½" x 2½"

E ½" x 10"

F ½" x 15"

H 1½" x 15"

J 2½" x 19"

L 3" x 24"

A

B

C

D 2" x 2"

You've Stolen My Heart!

Note: All measurements are finished measurements.

- *Medium red print for border K and L:* ½ yard. To get a top and bottom border, each 3" x 25", finished, cut two rectangles 3½" x 25½". To get two side borders, each 3" x 24", finished, cut two rectangles 3½" x 24½".
- *Backing:* 1 yard
- *Batting:* One crib/craft-size batt
- *Binding:* 115"

Fabric for Project #2
- *Blue background fabric (templates B, D, Q, and P):* assorted scraps or ⅜ yard. To get fabric prepared for assorted methods, cut 28 squares 4" x 4".
- *Red fabric for hearts (templates A and C) and four corner squares (template Q):* assorted scraps or ⅜ yard. To get fabric prepared for assorted methods, cut 28 squares 4" x 4".

- *Medium red solid for border E and F:* ¼ yard. To get a top and bottom border, each ½" x 10", finished, cut two rectangles 1" x 10½". To get two side borders ½" x 15", finished, cut two rectangles 1" x 15½".
- *Dark red print fabric for border G and H:* ¼ yard. To get a top and bottom border, each 1½" x 10", finished, cut two rectangles 2" x 10½". To get two side borders 1½" x 15", finished, cut two rectangles 2" x 15½".
- *Dark blue print for border I and J:* ¼ yard. To get a top and bottom border, each 2½" x 14", finished, cut two rectangles 3" x 14½". To get two side borders 2½" x 19", finished, cut two rectangles 3" x 19½".
- *Medium blue for the reverse appliqué border (template M):* ½ yard. Reverse appliqué the blue down to the red border which is solid red (½ yard) on the inside, red print (½ yard) on the outside.

PROJECT #2
Small quilt: "Be My Valentine."

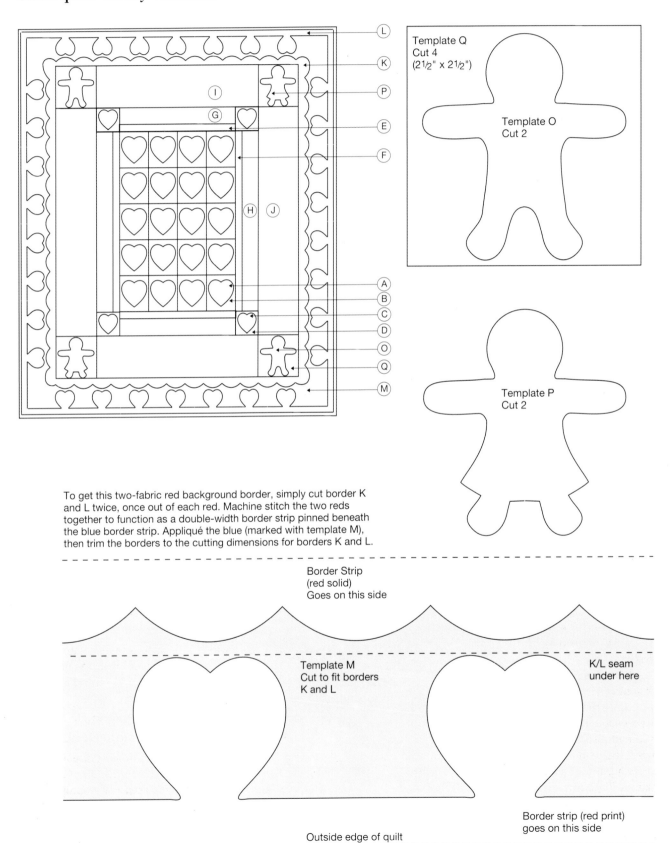

Template Q
Cut 4
(2½" x 2½")

Template O
Cut 2

Template P
Cut 2

To get this two-fabric red background border, simply cut border K and L twice, once out of each red. Machine stitch the two reds together to function as a double-width border strip pinned beneath the blue border strip. Appliqué the blue (marked with template M), then trim the borders to the cutting dimensions for borders K and L.

Border Strip
(red solid)
Goes on this side

Template M
Cut to fit borders
K and L

K/L seam
under here

Border strip (red print)
goes on this side

Outside edge of quilt

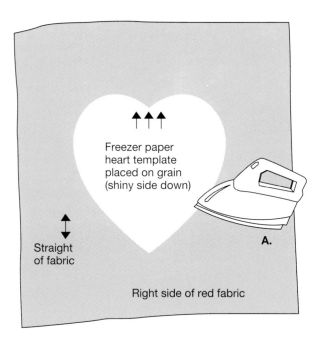

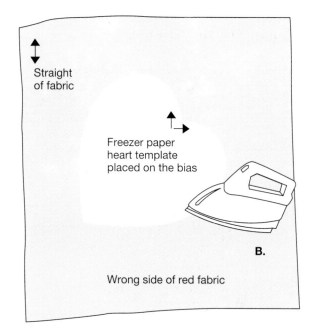

FIGURE 2-1A-B.

When hearts are cut on the straight of the fabric ("on grain"), the threads at the inward corner threaten to fray as they stick straight upwards from the deepest cut. There are some wonderful methods (#1, 2, and 3 for example) where you must place the hearts on the straight of the fabric. But where there's a choice, placing them on the bias of the fabric means that the threads at the inward point of the heart are heading in the direction you want them to turn under.

When hearts are cut on the bias, the threads at the heart's inward corner just naturally face away from the deepest part of the cut.

Other Supplies

- 1 yard polycoated freezer paper for cutting heart templates
- One file card to make a heart template for Method #9 (though if you like this method, white poster board works even better and the shapes are reusable)
- Small, fine craft paint brush for Method #9 (or use a cotton swab just to learn the method)
- Spray starch (not liquid starch, not powdered starch—it's the sewable character of spray starch that gives Method #9, Spray Appliqué, its catchy, but cryptic name)
- Gluestick
- White school paste for Method #10 (or try Sticky Stuff®, a new product welcomed because the surface it's applied to remains tacky—a template treated with it is both reusable and easy to remove)
- Self-stick adhesive label big enough to cut a heart from template A (if you like Method #10, you may want to buy sheets of uncut labels or stick-on shelf paper)
- Permanent Pigma Micron pen (.02 or .03) for writing
- Magic Sizing to stabilize the fabric for writing upon
- Fabric marking pencil
- Red thread to match the red hearts (and blue thread to match the background fabric for Method #3)

- One square 4" x 4" of fusible web (try Wonder-Under® or Aleene's™ Hot Stitch Fusible Web™)

Preparation

For efficiency, do all the preparation first, then concentrate on the lessons. Happily, this list of preparations will only take half-an-hour or so after you've gathered supplies. To keep track of what you've done, check off each preparation step as you do it. Then write a number on each item you prepare to correspond to the same number in the instructions.

1. Cut one window template each from templates B and D. (A window template is the piecing shape itself, with the appliqué motif cut out of it.) Cut one heart template each from A and C.

2. Cut five freezer paper hearts using template A.

3. Cut one template A heart out of the file card.

4. Make 24 pleasing color combination sets, pairing one 4" red appliqué fabric square with one 4" blue background square. Now you're ready to prepare the blocks for the actual sewing.

5. Draw template A on the smooth side of the 4" square of fusible web. Iron the whole square of fusible web (rough side down) to the wrong side of a square of

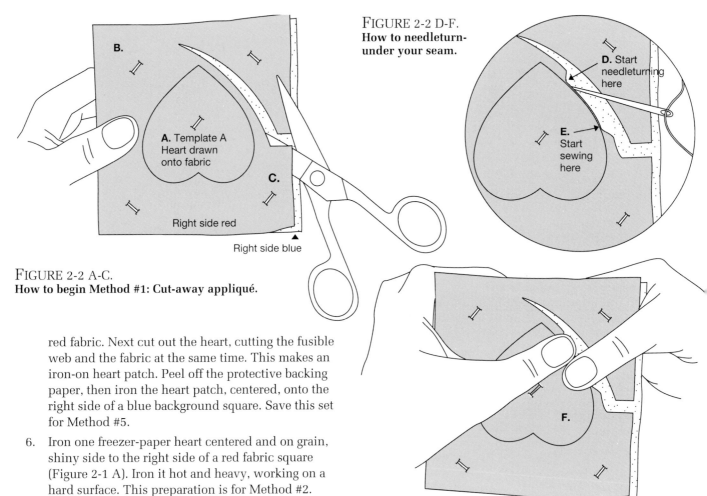

FIGURE 2-2 A-C.
How to begin Method #1: Cut-away appliqué.

FIGURE 2-2 D-F.
How to needleturn-under your seam.

red fabric. Next cut out the heart, cutting the fusible web and the fabric at the same time. This makes an iron-on heart patch. Peel off the protective backing paper, then iron the heart patch, centered, onto the right side of a blue background square. Save this set for Method #5.

6. Iron one freezer-paper heart centered and on grain, shiny side to the right side of a red fabric square (Figure 2-1 A). Iron it hot and heavy, working on a hard surface. This preparation is for Method #2.

7. Iron one freezer-paper heart centered and on the bias, shiny side to the right side of a red fabric square. This preparation is for Method #4.

8. Iron two freezer paper hearts (shiny side down), one each to the wrong side of two red squares. Place the hearts on the bias of the fabric (Figure 2-1 B). This preparation is for Methods #7 and #10.

Now, let's begin the how-to-appliqué lesson by making one heart at a time, using ten different methods to prepare appliqués for ten different hearts. Do the remaining hearts by using your favorite method(s). Undoubtedly the way you practice most will become the easiest one for you. But certain projects lend themselves more easily to one kind of appliqué than another—and you will know all ten ways very soon.

Techniques: Appliqué Methods with Seams Not Prepared Before Sewing

METHOD #1: CUT-AWAY APPLIQUÉ

In this method, cut just a little bit of the fabric at a time. When the cut section has been sewn, then cut a little bit more. Let's follow this method, step by step, on the first heart.

1. Draw template A, centered on grain, on the right side of a red fabric square (Figure 2-2 A).

2. Pin this marked square of red to a square of blue (right sides of both fabrics facing you). Pin the squares together in five places: one in each corner, and one in the center. Put the pins on the back so the thread doesn't catch on the pins as you sew (Figure 2-2 B). **Note:** For a larger cut-away appliqué, use three more pins right where you are sewing. Whenever these pins are in the way, move them on. They replace the need for basting.

FIGURE 2-2 G.
How to needleturn an outward point.

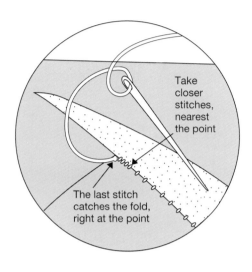

Take closer stitches, nearest the point

The last stitch catches the fold, right at the point

FIGURE 2-2 H.
**Change the direction of your cut. Trim seam for 2"
up the (now right-hand) side of the heart.**

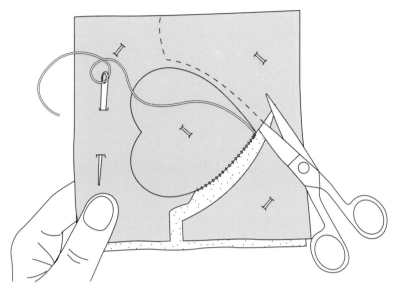

3. Thread a #11 Sharp needle with an 18" knotted thread in the color of the appliqué (the red fabric).
4. Begin at the easiest place on the heart—high on its side. Hold the heart as shown (Figure 2-2 C). Cut the red fabric only, trimming a seam to ³⁄₁₆" away from the drawn heart. Cut (from half-an-inch to an inch) beyond its point.
5. Needleturn under the seam. To do this, catch the seam with the needle, pull it under towards you, and hold it under with your thumb. Start to needle turn about ¾" above where you want to sew (Figure 2-2 D). Using the shank of the needle, roll under the seam by sliding the needle under along the turn line, pulling it towards you (Figure 2-2 E). Take both hands and fingerpress under this seam so that it stays prepared (Figure 2-2 F).
6. Start sewing (appliquéing) the edge under, using the tack stitch.

Note: Aim to take no fewer than 10 stitches per inch. Some antique appliqué was done with a tiny seam (close to ¹⁄₁₆") having 15 to 20 stitches per inch. But with our comfortable ³⁄₁₆" seam, 10 or so stitches per inch will do nicely. If your stitches are fine and they keep the seam under smoothly, then they're close enough. Remember to tug each stitch slightly as you pull it through. When stitches show too much it is often because they are loose.

7. When you're ¼" from the heart's outward point, take close stitches all the way to the point. You will be tucking the left side of the heart's seam against those stitches and you don't want the right side of the point to bulge out. Bring your last stitch up, catching the fold right at the point (Figure 2-2 G). Once you reach the point where the two drawn lines

touch, put down the needle and pick up the scissors. Cut about 2" up what is now the right side of the heart (Figure 2-2 H). If you master the turning of this point, you will have the touch for turning even the sharpest of nonprepared points. Nonprepared points (also called needleturned

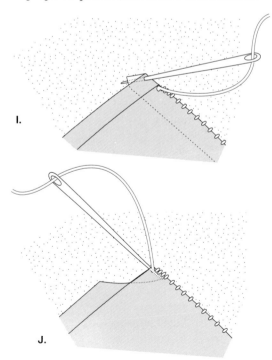

I.

J.

FIGURE 2-2 I-J.
**Catch both seams on the tip of the needle. The secret is to
insert just the needle's tip, close to the raw edges and close
to the fold. Then, scrape the seams around and under
(against your forefinger, pressing up from behind the background fabric). The needle stops at the already-sewn seam.**

FIGURE 2-2 K.

Pinch the point to press in the turn. Then tug your thread to pull the tucked point into line. This pull may have an extraordinary effect! Detail: Complete the stitch at the point.

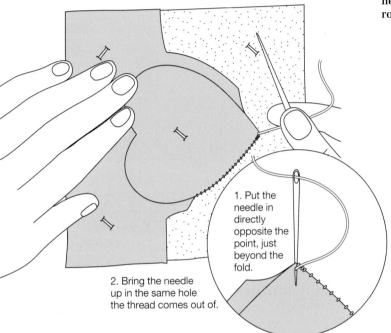

1. Put the needle in directly opposite the point, just beyond the fold.

2. Bring the needle up in the same hole the thread comes out of.

FIGURE 2-2 L.

Seam widths: The larger (³⁄₁₆") seam helps at an outward point where a tiny seam might disintegrate into fray in the turning under. That same more generous ³⁄₁₆" seam helps keep under the turned sides of an inward point, as at the top of your heart. But on a curve, a finer ⅛" seam aids a smoothly rounded seam.

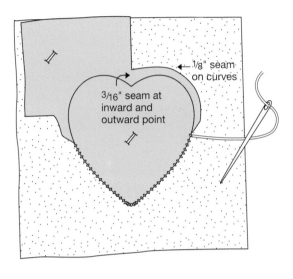

← ⅛" seam on curves

³⁄₁₆" seam at inward and outward point

points) are all basically done the following way, no matter which method you are using.

8. Now you're ready to turn the heart's point under. Catch the top seam and the tucked-under seam, pressing this loaded needle against the background cloth (Figure 2-2 I-J). Tighten the blue background fabric over your left forefinger so that the background fabric remains still while you scrape those seams to their resting place underneath the point. Pinch the seam to crease this turned point under. Next, tug the thread to pull the seams smoothly into line at the very point (Figure 2-2 K). Now complete your stitch at the point. Re-enter the background fabric just beyond the point (not under the fold) and come back up in exactly the same hole the thread comes up through in step #7 (Figure 2-2 K, detail). Pull the stitch tight.

9. Once the point is turned in step #8, you simply have to tuck and stitch, tuck and stitch, in a nice smooth line leading away from the point. On a very sharp narrow point, you'll need something stronger than a needle to do the initial tucking. A round wooden toothpick or the tips of embroidery scissors work nicely. If the point is getting frayed while you try to turn it, switch immediately to these larger tools for that job, too. If the point is very sharp and narrow and you have to trim off more seam, do it right after step #8, since then the tricky part of the point will have been sewn. But on today's heart in

this lesson, there is no need to trim the point. There is plenty of room and the point will be stronger for having all of the ³⁄₁₆" seam left in it.

10. Sew what is now the right side of the heart as far as possible until you need to cut further. Then cut to (but not into) the halfway spot at the top of the heart's inward point (Figure 2-2 L). This time, as

FIGURE 2-2 M.

The secret of a smooth curve: In needleturning the right heart shoulder, you're turning a gentle curve. Your left thumb holds the turned under edge as you sew towards it. The secret to not getting points on your curves is never to sew right up to your thumb. Always stop sewing about ¼" short of your thumb so that you can fan out the seam underneath the fold. This allows the fabric to change directions as the curve is turned. This method uses a fine seam on the curve, but no clipping on an outside curve.

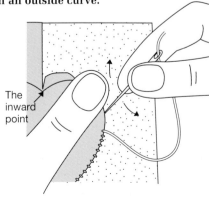

The inward point

FIGURE 2-2 N.
Turning an inward point. Begin turning the inward point when you're ½" away from it. Lay the needle over the right seam flap, under the left.

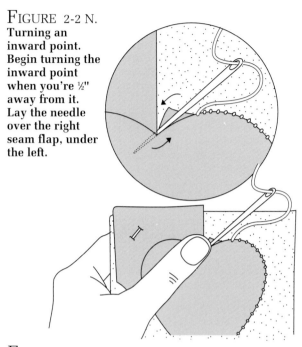

FIGURE 2-2 O.
Pinch the needle with your left hand. With your right, catch the right seam flap on the side of the needle and pull it under the heart. Keep fingerpressing and sew right up to your thumb.

FIGURE 2-2 P.
Stitching an inward point.

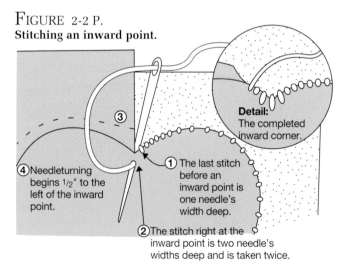

④ Needleturning begins ½" to the left of the inward point.

③

① The last stitch before an inward point is one needle's width deep.

② The stitch right at the inward point is two needle's widths deep and is taken twice.

Detail:
The completed inward corner.

you cut the curved seam on the heart's shoulder, reduce the seam to about ⅛" away from the drawn seam line. Since outward curves aren't clipped in cut-away appliqué, a slightly narrower seam makes turning the curve easier.

11. When you are at the top of the heart's curve, clip the inward point, giving equal seam allowance to both sides of the heart. Cut a straight line, perpendicular to the point. How deep? The rule is always "Clip to, but not through, the drawn line." (See the inward point in Figure 2-2 M.) Don't touch that clip further until you have sewn up to ½" from the inward point.

Note: Here's a suggestion from prizewinning appliquér, Charlotte Warr Andersen. To avoid fray at inward points, trace the cutting line with a pin dipped in Fray Check™. Wait until this dries, then do your cutting.

12. When ½" away, tuck the seam under at the inside point. Lay the side of the needle over the right flap of the seam. The needle's tip will lie between the heart appliqué and the background fabric, able to move freely (Figure 2-2 N). Press the needle between your left thumb (on top of the needle in the crack) and your forefinger (under the block) (Figure 2-2 O). With the shank of the needle, pull the flap under towards you. Keep your fingers pinched while you sew up to your thumb. When you've reached it, lift your thumb up to see how you're doing. If there is a bit of fray, avoid sewing it. Generally, it is easier for a right-handed person to turn fray under to the left of the inward point.

13. The last stitch taken (before the deep cut of the inward "V") should be slightly deeper than the ones you've been taking. If you lay a needle on the folded seam, the width of the needle's shank is how deep this stitch should be (Figure 2-2 P). And the stitch right at the point should be twice that distance (two needles' widths) from the raw edge. Take this double-deep stitch twice. Put the needle in just under the edge of the red where you went in before. Bring it up through the red exactly where you came out before. You've just stitched a loop which will lasso the raw edge under when you pull it tight. Do so now. Take one more slightly long stitch on the left side of the inward point. It should match the one on the right side. But before you take it, cut the left side of the heart.

FIGURE 2-2 Q.
A blanket stitch can secure an inward point. If you want something wider than a single stitch to secure an inward point, take a blanket stitch at the deepest point.

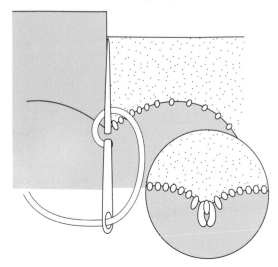

FIGURE 2-3 A-C.
Heart being sewn by Method #2: Cut-away appliqué with freezer paper on the top.

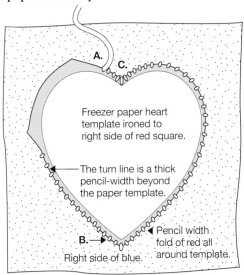

14. Next, begin the needleturn for the left side ½" above the turned point. If there's a bit of fray, try sweeping it under with an assertive turn here, carrying the needle's motion right up to the sewn point. If that doesn't work, tuck under the fray with a round wooden toothpick or the tips of embroidery scissors. Now you can take your slightly longer stitch immediately to the left of the point (Figure 2-2 P, detail). Continue sewing the heart to completion. If it looks decent, imagine what a looker heart number twenty will be with all that practice in between!

METHOD #2: CUT-AWAY APPLIQUÉ WITH FREEZER PAPER ON THE TOP

This method follows the same steps for cutting and sewing detailed in Method #1, but now you will have a freezer-paper template ironed to the right side of the fabric (Figure 2-1 A). What's the advantage? The paper heart marks the pattern in a clear, visible way, and acts as a "third hand" holding the appliqué smooth and flat. It gives a sharp line against which to turn the seam under. And it highlights the narrow fold, so that where to tack stitch catching the fold is clearly visible (Figure 2-3 A). Important: When you use any of the freezer-paper methods, remember the turn line is not the paper's edge itself. Rather, the turn line is an imaginary pencil line "drawn" around the freezer paper shape. This "line" will help you know how far to cut for outward points (to where the two imaginary lines touch) and how far to sew for inward points (to, but not through the drawn line). (See Figure 2-3 B and C.) If you slip and

FIGURE 2-4 A-B.
Cutting the appliqué squares to size for patchwork: There's a neat trick to trimming the background blocks. Place the window template B so that its cutout heart outlines the stitches on the back of a completed heart block. Draw around template B's rectangular shape.

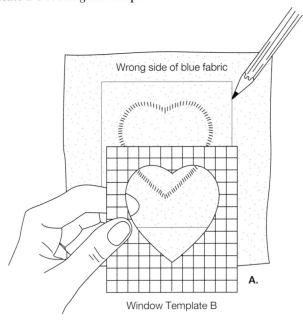

The drawn line is the sewing line for joining the patchwork rectangles together by hand or machine. Now cut a neat ¼" seam allowance beyond the drawn edge to leave your seam allowance.

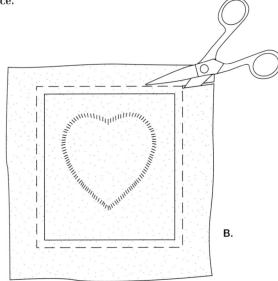

Now (Figure 2-4 B) the block is the correct size with the appliqué heart perfectly centered in it. Notice that in some prepared appliqué methods, the hearts can become a bit skewed on the block. Just use this nifty window-template to center the heart and cut the block to size. Since small separate appliqué pieces tend to turn on the background as you sew, pin them with more than one pin (one pin acts as a pivot), or baste them. Even basting with big stitches should suffice.

cut too close at the inward point, you can stitch through the paper. It's simply easier to see what you're doing if you keep that cut a thick pencil line away from the paper.

1. Take the red square from preparation step #6 and pin it to a blue background, right sides of both facing you. To sew this heart, follow the steps in Method #1, reviewing them first. Remember, all the rules for cut-away appliqué can be summarized in two sentences: Never cut around a point, but rather cut beyond (up to 1" beyond) a point; and, never change the direction of your cut until the first side is sewn.

2. When the heart is finished, you should see a fine fold of fabric outlining the heart (Figure 2-3 A). Now pull off the freezer paper heart, and admire your work! This is my very favorite way to appliqué. When you see Method #2 listed first among the possibilities for the projects that follow, you'll know why. There are, however, other charming projects where one of the methods yet-to-come is simply better—and equally fun. (See Figure 2-4 for how to cut your appliqués to size for patchwork.)

FIGURE 2-5 A-G.

Method #3: Reverse appliqué. The appliqué is done on the blue, turning the seam back to reveal the red heart underneath.

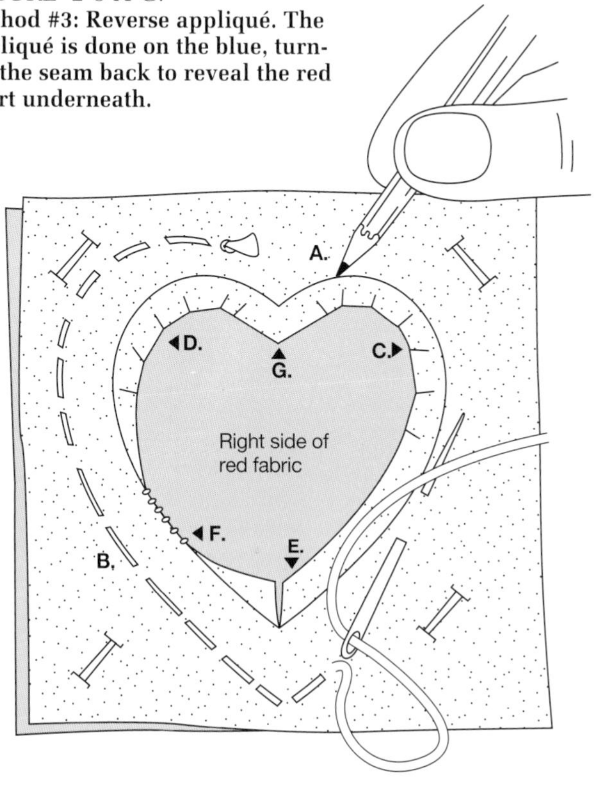

Right side of red fabric

METHOD #3: REVERSE APPLIQUÉ

In reverse appliqué, you turn the blue background cloth under to expose the red heart fabric which has been pinned beneath it. So it is just the opposite (the "reverse") of an appliqué where the shape itself is sewn, seams under, to a background. There is less fabric to tuck under the curves in reverse appliqué, so this way, curves should be quicker and easier. Thus reverse appliqué is often used for such curvacious projects as feather borders. There's a great border to try this technique on in Project #20. Reverse appliqué only becomes easy with practice, so do give it a chance.

1. Using template A, draw a heart on the right side of a blue square. Pin it to a red square, right sides of both facing you (Figure 2-5 A).

2. Baste the heart ½" outside the turn line (Figure 2-5 B). This is not crucial, but it will remind you not to pull the seam further under on one shoulder of the heart than the other. There is a tendency to do this in reverse appliqué, but the resulting lopsidedness is only a problem on a shape (like the heart) that is supposed to be symmetrical. On something asymmetrical, like the petals in Project #20, you could pin only and not baste.

3. Trim the blue (only) back to ³⁄₁₆" from the turn line (Figure 2-5 C).

4. At the deepest points on the inward curves, clip the seam allowance two-thirds of the way to the drawn line. You are easing the seam just enough to allow it to be tucked back (Figure 2-5 D). Clip right to the turn line at the inward corner at the bottom of the heart (Figure 2-5 E).

5. Thread your needle with 18" (knotted) of blue thread, the color of the background fabric. Begin sewing on the left side (Figure 2-5 F). Use the tack stitch to come up through the red, under the edge of the blue folded seam. Exit the blue, just catching the fold. Follow the same directions as in Method #1, but now your outward point is at the top of the heart (Figure 2-5 G), the inward point at the bottom.

6. When the appliqué is complete, go to the underneath side. Pull out the basting and trim back the red to ¼" beyond the seam. If the appliqué had been white or another see-through color (instead of blue), you could cut back the red fabric a bit further so it's hidden underneath the white seam. If show-through is unavoidable (as it sometimes is), take pains to cut a respectably even seam.

METHOD #4: NEEDLETURN APPLIQUÉ

In the first three methods, you have been using the needle to turn the seam under as you sew. You have been doing "needleturn appliqué," preparing the seam by tucking it

FIGURE 2-6 A-B.
Method #5: Fused appliqué with a blanket-stitch finish.

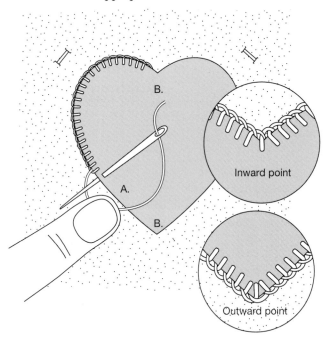

under with the needle. It's probably the oldest and most universal way to appliqué. Needleturn can also be done on appliqués cut out all at once as opposed to having the seam cut a little bit at a time.

Let's try simple needleturn on still another heart. There are really three possible preparation methods for a needle-turned heart. You could draw the heart, trim the seam, and sew it. Or, you could have a freezer-paper heart ironed to the wrong side of the fabric, trim the seam, and needleturn the seam under against the sharp ridge of the paper template. (You would have to remove the paper before you finished sewing, or remove it by cutting out the back after you finished sewing.) The third preparation method uses freezer paper on top. It's the one I prefer, and this preparation combined with needleturn is what we'll refer to hereafter as Method #4.

1. Use the red square with a paper heart on top from preparation step #7. Trim the seam all around to ³⁄₁₆". Pin (or baste) the heart, centered, on a square of background blue.

2. Hold the heart point away from you. Begin on the right side, on the flatish portion of the heart. Proceed as in Method #1, beginning with step #5. When finished, you should see a very narrow fold of fabric outlining the paper heart. Now peel off the freezer-paper pattern. **Note:** If you've been overzealous in ironing down the freezer paper and it shreds when you pull it off, here's what to do. Reheat the paper by ironing it lightly. With tweezers, lift up the paper in a nonshredded area and pull towards the shredded area. If a bit is left, rub it with a damp terry

washcloth. More commonly, the paper lifts because it has not been ironed on hot and hard enough. Try it again, with a very hot iron, forcefully. Important: Pretest by ironing a sample to the fabric first.

METHOD #5: FUSED APPLIQUÉ WITH A BLANKET-STITCH FINISH

Ah! Modern technology makes this kind of appliqué fun and virtually foolproof. It is another of my favorites. Use the fusible web-backed heart from preparation step #5. It has already been fused to a blue background. You'll sew over this fused edge, binding it with the blanket stitch. This method is a real find for sewing fabric designs based on Pennsylvania Dutch frakturs. (It was used for all or part of Projects #8, #9, #19, and #24.) The blanket stitch is always both functional and decorative.

1. Use either a double sewing thread, or a heavier thread like a single strand of embroidery floss. Do the blanket stitch, working towards you (Figure 2-6 A). The needle takes a bite from the inside of the heart and comes up just outside the fused edge. Your thumb holds the tail of the thread down, so that the needle comes up over it and, when pulled, completes the stitch.

2. Figure 2-6 B shows how the stitch goes around an inward and an outward point. Because the fusible bonds the raw edge, you don't have to bind the edge with close stitches. About eight to ten stitches per inch works well. The beauty of the stitch is in having the stitches equidistant and all the same length.

MACHINE APPLIQUÉ HINT: *Fusing the raw-edged appliqués to the background fabric is also a great way to prepare for machine stitching with the satin stitch. Machine satin stitch over an iron-on fusible would be an acceptable way to do any of the projects in this book. For the finer-scale projects, use a narrower stitch. I always use an exact color match or a shade darker, and put my stitches as close together as the machine allows. Fusible is less successful for layered appliqué since more than one fused layer makes the fabric too stiff for a quilt top.*

Techniques: Appliqué Methods with Seams Prepared Before Sewing

In Methods #6 through #10, the seam is turned under and attached to the heart shape before it is appliquéd down. People who like these seams-prepared methods argue that preparing the seam first makes the appliqué easier, and, in some cases, faster. These methods are particularly useful

FIGURE 2-7 A-D.
Method #6: Baste-and-turn appliqué.

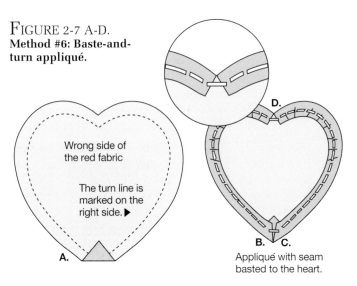

Wrong side of the red fabric

The turn line is marked on the right side. ▶

A.

B. C.

D.

Appliqué with seam basted to the heart.

for seeing what the finished appliqué will look like before it's sewn. This helps you judge the effects of color and design. Turning the edge before you sew may also be a quicker, easier way to get smooth curves and perfect points. It seems particularly worthwhile to try a prepared method when you're dealing repeatedly with the same shape, as with these hearts. Three of these methods involve sewing with the freezer-paper template left on. Note that whichever way you use freezer paper (including Methods #2 and #4), the paper keeps the appliqués from shrinking when you sew. Thus the prepared methods (#7, #8, and #10) are excellent when you need to mark your background cloth for a more complex design. With these last three methods, you can see the background markings (since the seam is already turned) and the appliqués (held in shape by the paper) won't shrink to expose those marking lines when sewn.

METHOD #6: BASTE-AND-TURN APPLIQUÉ

Most people who were taught to appliqué in the early to middle decades of this century learned this method. It works well, but the preparation is quite time-consuming and can be discouraging if there is much of it to do.

1. Draw the heart on the right side of the red fabric. Trim the seam allowance off to ¾6". Now turn the heart over so that you are looking at the wrong side of the fabric. You will be pulling the seam to the back of the shape, fingerpressing under the seam at the drawn line, then sewing it in place. Though you don't have to, you can also prepare the turn line itself. Here are two methods. Mark the turn line on the wrong side (only) of the fabric. Next, echo the drawn line with a continuous row of tight machine straight-stitching just to the raw edge side of the line. Or, you can "score" the turn line, working on a cutting mat or a pad of paper. To score, press the turn line into the fabric by going over it with the

back of a large darning needle or awl.

2. Prepare the point seam first. Put a dab of glue (from a gluestick) on the seam at the point. Press the point seam back against the heart (Figure 2-7 A). Put another dab of glue on top of this turned point to hold the sides as you fold them in to the center. Now press first the left seam to the center (Figure 2-7 B), then the right. You have a perfectly turned point (Figure 2-7 C). The point is turned this same way on all the prepared appliqué methods.

3. Now baste this turned seam to the appliqué. Sew the straighter part of the heart first. Your basting stitches will run along the middle of the seam.

4. On the curved "shoulders" of the heart, fingerpress the curve first, fanning (but not clipping) the excess fabric under smoothly as you sew.

5. Clip the inward point, then fingerpress the seam under and continue basting in the middle of the seam (Figure 2-7 D). Don't try to sew into the inward point now. The inward point is a raw edge and must be rolled under with a series of three longer tack stitches as described in Method #1, step #13. Stitch all inward points this way.

6. When the seam is all basted under, baste the heart (seam side down) to the right side of the background fabric. It's now all ready to appliqué by the tack or blind stitch.

FIGURE 2-8 A-C.
Method #7: English paper method.

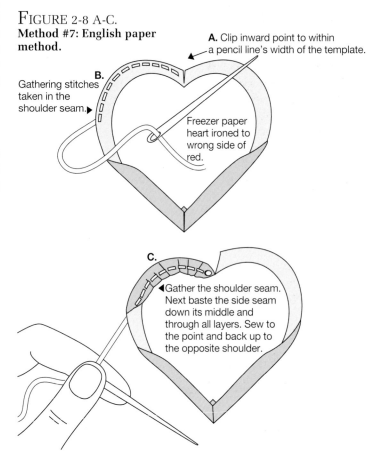

A. Clip inward point to within a pencil line's width of the template.

B. Gathering stitches taken in the shoulder seam. ▶

Freezer paper heart ironed to wrong side of red.

C. ◀Gather the shoulder seam. Next baste the side seam down its middle and through all layers. Sew to the point and back up to the opposite shoulder.

FIGURE 2-8 D-I.

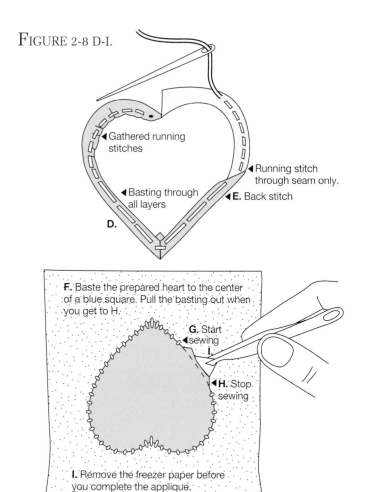

F. Baste the prepared heart to the center of a blue square. Pull the basting out when you get to H.

G. Start sewing

H. Stop sewing

I. Remove the freezer paper before you complete the appliqué.

METHOD #7: ENGLISH PAPER METHOD

In this method, the seam allowance is basted over a paper template. The template gives a nice sharp edge against which to turn the seam allowance under and the basting keeps the turned seam in place. Many people use a light paper like photocopy or typing paper for this method. I prefer freezer paper because it sticks temporarily to the fabric and makes the basting easy.

1. Take one freezer-paper heart ironed to the wrong side of the fabric (preparation step #8). Trim the seam allowance to ¼" from the edge of the paper.

2. Prepare the point as in Method #6, step #2 (Figure 2-7 A-C).

3. Clip the heart at its inward corner to within a wide pencil line of the paper (Figure 2-8 A).

4. With a well-knotted thread, do running stitches through the seam only (not through the paper). Stitch for about 1½" from the center cut to over the left shoulder of the heart. Stitch closer to the raw edge than to the paper template (Figure 2-8 B). Pull the thread tight to gather your running stitches over the curve (Figure 2-8 C). Next, continue to take running stitches, but now go through the paper. These are

longer basting stitches sewn down the middle of the seam through all layers (Figure 2-8 D). (The gathering done here is optional. For most shapes, simply baste all the seams through the paper.)

5. Sew down to the point and back up the right-hand side until you are at the bottom of the opposite shoulder of the heart (Figure 2-8 E). Backstitch once, then do the running stitches (through the seam only) until you are at the heart's inward point. Pull the thread to gather the curve and finish by tacking the thread off on this right side of the inward point. Baste this prepared heart onto the center of the 4" square (Figure 2-8 F).

6. Appliqué the heart using the tack stitch. Begin just to the right of the point (Figure 2-8 G). Stop sewing 1" from where you started (Figure 2-8 H). Pull out all the basting. Reach under the appliqué and loosen the freezer paper with tweezers, then pull out the paper template (Figure 2-8 I). Now stitch the remaining seam down. You can also remove the paper by slitting the background fabric to within ¼" of the seam, loosening the freezer paper with tweezers, and pulling it out. Or, carefully trim the background fabric to within ¼" from the seam and remove the paper from the back. This gives appliqués a flat look, like patchwork. It's done to make the appliqués easier to quilt through. I myself only cut out the back on large-scale machine appliqués.

METHOD #8: FREEZER PAPER INSIDE (WITH SEAMS IRONED OVER IT)

Use freezer paper inside the appliqué, shiny side up, so that the ironed-down seams adhere to its plastic coating. When people talk about doing freezer-paper appliqué, they are probably talking about this method. It is the original freezer-paper method devised by Anne Oliver.

1. Pin a freezer-paper heart template (shiny side towards you) on the bias, on the wrong side of a 4" square of red fabric.

FIGURE 2-9 A-E.
Method #8: Freezer paper inside (with seams ironed over it)

B.

A. Freezer paper heart pinned shiny side up

C. At the inward point, clip to, but not through, the imaginary pencil line around the heart template.

E.

Freezer paper heart shiny side up.

D.

2. Trim to ¼" seam allowance beyond the heart template (Figure 2-9 A). Make a prepared point (see Method #6, step #2), but on this one, iron the point back over the freezer-paper heart to start. The heat will seal the point seam to the paper (Figure 2-9 B). Then carry on with Method #6, step #2.

3. Now that the paper is well-anchored to the fabric and will not move out of register, you can clip the inward point. How far? Clip to, but not through, the imaginary line which outlines the paper. Don't clip right to the paper. Make sure your clip is straight to the line and gives equal seam allowance to both sides (Figure 2-9 C).

4. Fold the left lobe of the heart back to get it out of the way (Figure 2-9 D). "Heat baste" the curved seam by turning the seam and pressing it down with the tip of the iron at roughly half-inch intervals. Now that you've got the seam turning, iron the right seam tightly against the right inward point of the heart Figure 2-9 E). Finish ironing the curved seam to the freezer paper. Now fold the right lobe of the heart down and repeat this process.

5. When the heart is fully prepared over freezer paper, iron it down to the center right side of the blue fabric. There is enough shiny surface still exposed on the template to adhere to the blue when ironed. (However, I personally prefer to pin or baste the shape on.)

6. Begin sewing the heart. Complete the heart the same as you did in Method #7, step #6.

MACHINE APPLIQUÉ HINT: *Method #8 is a good way to prepare your shapes for machine appliqué using the blind hem-stitch and clear nylon monofilament thread. Method #8 turns the seam quickly, and even if a tiny bite of the paper is caught, it still pulls out easily through a slit in the background cloth. In addition, the exposed freezer paper on the wrong side of the appliqué can be "basted" to the background fabric by ironing it down for a smooth, stable—but temporary—hold so that you can machine stitch the turn line easily. Jeannie Koch uses this method, taking a final press on the right side of the turned shape to ensure sharply creased curves, then pulling the paper out before even pinning the appliqué to the background. Perhaps spray starch with that final press would keep the crease even better. Another popular, but more time-consuming, preparation for blind hemstitching is machine stitching the appliqué (right side down) to a nonwoven "dryer sheet" (designed to combat static in the clothes dryer). Having straight-stitched the turn line, trim the dryer sheet seam to ⅛", slit its center, and pull the appliqué shape through until it's right-side out. Set your iron on low for synthetics and press the turned seams from the back over a towel. Use a pressing cloth to protect the nylon thread when ironing monofilament-sewn appliqués. If you like, trim out both the cloth and the dryer sheet from behind the appliqué.*

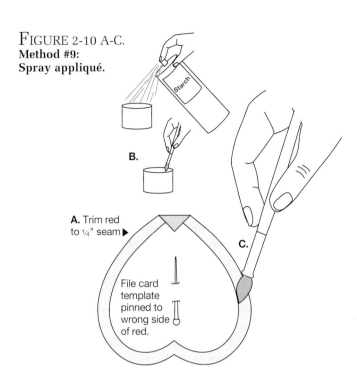

FIGURE 2-10 A-C.
Method #9:
Spray appliqué.

B.

A. Trim red to ¼" seam ▶

C.

File card template pinned to wrong side of red.

METHOD #9: SPRAY APPLIQUÉ

Using spray starch to fix the turned seam is another way to prepare appliqué. People who like this method argue that it's easy on the fabric. It uses preparation step #3, and here's how it's done.

1. Pin (or glue) the file card heart template, on the bias, to the wrong side of a 4" red square.

2. Trim to ¼" seam allowance around the template (Figure 2-10 A). Spray ¼" of liquid spray starch into the spray can's cap (Figure 2-10 B). Using a fine brush (or a cotton swab), paint this starch onto the heart's turn line. Follow the edge of the file card, but avoid softening the paper by wetting it (Figure 2-10 C).

3. Prepare the point as in Method #6, step #2.

4. Iron the bottom sides of the heart up and over. Hold the iron for a few seconds, until the starch dries. When done, clip the inward point to a pencil-line width from the template. Iron the sides of the inward point over, then the curves.

5. When the seams are turned, iron the heart, seams down, from the front with a spray of starch. Remove the template and sew the heart to the square of blue. **Note:** Alternatively, you could use a freezer-paper template and Method #8 to turn all the heart's seams. Simply finish by starching and ironing from the front, and remove the paper template.

FIGURE 2-11 A-C.
Method #10: Freezer paper inside with adhesive (or appliqué with self-stick paper)

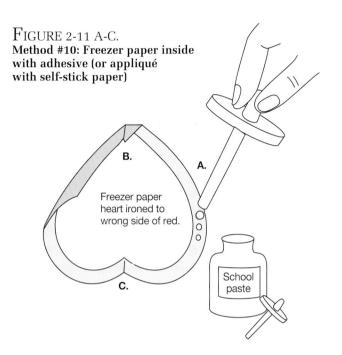

Freezer paper heart ironed to wrong side of red.

School paste

METHOD #10: FREEZER PAPER INSIDE WITH ADHESIVE (OR APPLIQUÉ WITH SELF-STICK PAPER)

Advocates of this method like it because it is all sit-down work after the simple process of ironing the freezer-paper template to the wrong side of the fabric. Use either school paste (Anna Holland's method), Sticky Stuff, or a spray glue (M. Grumbacher® Spray Adhesive™ or Spray Mount® Artist's Adhesive) as an adhesive with the freezer paper. Alternatively, use self-adhesive papers in the same manner to catch and hold the turned seam.

1. Use a freezer-paper heart ironed to the wrong side of the fabric (preparation step #8). Trim fabric to ¼" seam. Apply a narrow margin of adhesive around the edge of the freezer-paper heart (Figure 2-11 A).

2. Prepare the point as in Method #6, step #2. Fingerpress the seams of the outward point to the paper (Figure 2-11 B). Now that things won't move, clip the inward point to a pencil line away from the paper (Figure 2-11 C).

3. Fingerpress under the curves and inward point to complete the heart. Appliqué the heart to the blue square. Leave the paper in until you're ready to assemble the quilt. The school paste (which never did hold the kids' pictures together!) should have lost its grip by then. At that point, trim the back ground fabric out to ¼" from the seam and pull the paper out. If you use Sticky Stuff for holding the turned seam, the paper should also be easily removable. If it intrigues you, try yet another heart cut from a self-stick label. Pin it sticky side up to the wrong side of a red heart cut ¼" larger. Peel off half the protective paper at a time. Press the seams to the adhesive, and continue from step #2.

MACHINE *APPLIQUÉ* HINT: *Professional quiltmaker Jeanne Elliott blind hem-appliquéd Project #21 on her Bernina® #1230. Innovatively, she used the preparation for Method #10 trying both Sticky Stuff and spray adhesive. She laid all the hearts (with the freezer paper ironed on the wrong side) on newspaper and sprayed both the paper templates and the exposed (wrong) sides of the seams at the same time. Turning (and even repositioning) the seam was easy. Moreover, the now-sticky paper adhered to the background block for machining with no pins. Cutting the back and pulling out the paper was a snap. The spray adhesive both turned the seam and served to baste the appliqué to the background fabric.*

Now that you've completed all ten hearts, you've learned a lot—and your stitches have probably improved to boot. Congratulations! That's the way it is with appliqué: you just get better and better. Now it's time to think about how to do the rest of the blocks and how to finish your quilt top. My choice for completing these particular blocks would be Method #8. Since the heart shape is repeated over and over again, the ironing preparation is worth your while.

With the hearts completed, you have a choice of finishing your blocks into Project #1 or #2. The differences are just in the corner blocks and in the more demanding outside borders of Project #2. The assembly sequence for both quilts is simple. Do all the appliqué first, sew the trimmed blocks together in vertical rows, then sew the vertical rows to each other. Next sew the border corner blocks to the horizontal borders. Attach the inner borders to the quilt center, beginning with the vertical ones, then the horizontal ones. Repeat for all four borders. Make a top/batting/backing "sandwich"; quilt, and then bind. Now you're off and stitching!

WRITING ON CLOTH WITH A PERMANENT PEN:
To inscribe "You've Stolen My Heart!" (or any calligraphy on these projects), follow these steps:

1. *Stiffen the fabric by spraying its back with Magic Sizing, then ironing it. Or, iron freezer paper to the wrong side of the heart to stiffen it.*

2. *Working on a lightbox, trace the template A calligraphy onto the white heart. If you trace it in fine pencil first, go over it with a black Pigma Micron pen (.03 or .05).*

3. *Go back over the letters to thicken. Iron to set. For a heavier pen line on Project #14, use a black Pilot SC-UF pen. The Magic Sizing helps inhibit this heavier pen from bleeding.*

CHAPTER 3

Dutch Bulbs a-Bloomin'

More Techniques and an Introduction to the Projects

T his chapter's floral patterns are variations on traditional appliqué designs. Because of their Pennsylvania Dutch flavor, I've called them "Dutch Bulbs a-Bloomin'." We'll start with Version I, a pleasant way to learn a more challenging level of appliqué than the heart shape presented in Chapter 2. Special techniques taught in this chapter include using a marked background, doing layered appliqué, making superfine stems (Method #11), producing perfect grapes (Method #12), and mastering dimensional appliqué (Method #13, to make a baker's dozen!).

PROJECT #3
Pillow: "Dutch Bulbs a-Bloomin' Version I."
16" x 16".
Traditional pattern.

PROJECT #4
Pillow: "Dutch Bulbs a-Bloomin' Version II."
16" x 16".
Traditional pattern.

PROJECT #5
Pillow: "Dutch Bulbs a-Bloomin' Version III."
16" x 16".
"Winding Rose," designed by Ellen Peters.

Appliqué Methods: Method #8 for the flowers, Method #4 for the leaves. While you could choose others, these two offer the best lesson since they combine two very different methods in using a marked background.

Appliqué Ease Level: Moderately Easy

Fabric
- *Background fabric:* ½ yard white. Cut one 16½" square; ½" seams are included.
- *Flowers:* ¼ yard each of four shades of lavender
- *Leaves:* ¼ yard each of two shades of green
- *Edging:* optional
- *Folded ribbon flower centers:* (yardage based on 4½"

per flower of 1½"-wide rayon ribbon) ¼ yard each of dark blue, light blue, purple, and pink. ("French Wire Ribbon," which shades from light to dark, was used in the models. For purchasing information, contact Quilter's Resources, P. O. Box 148850, Chicago, IL 60614.)
- *Backing:* ½ yard

Other Supplies
- Freezer paper (for Methods #4 and #8)
- 16" pillow form or other stuffing
- Two 8½" strips of ¾"-wide masking tape. Use this as a pattern to cut the stem. Press the 8½" strips onto the bias of a green fabric. Cut around the tape, then remove it, leaving two 8½" x ¾" strips of bias-cut green for making superfine stems (Figure 3-1 A).

Assembly
Mark the background. Prepare templates A (Version I) and D (Version I) with freezer paper inside, according to Method #8 in Chapter 2. Prepare the leaves with freezer paper on the top for needleturn by Method #4. Appliqué the pillow top first, then quilt it. Back and finish the pillow according to taste.

Marking the background: When a design involves multiple shapes, some spare background marking helps. To begin, iron the 16½" square into quarters and then eighths for placement guidelines shown on the pattern. Next, place the fabric over the pattern and lightly mark one-quarter of the block at a time. Draw just the positioning marks given on this chapter's pattern pieces: bullets, arrows, dashed lines. These minimal markings are much safer than drawing out the whole design, where some lines may show in the end.

Layering: In the simplest appliqué, the separate shapes do not touch each other. When appliqué shapes do touch (as on our pillow), one shape actually lies under another shape, or is "layered" under another. Which shape goes on top and which on the bottom usually depends on the design and what looks best. In general, shapes overlap by ¼". Seams lying completely underneath another appliqué

PROJECT #3
**Pillow: "Dutch Bulbs a-Bloomin'
Version I."**
16" x 16".
Traditional pattern.

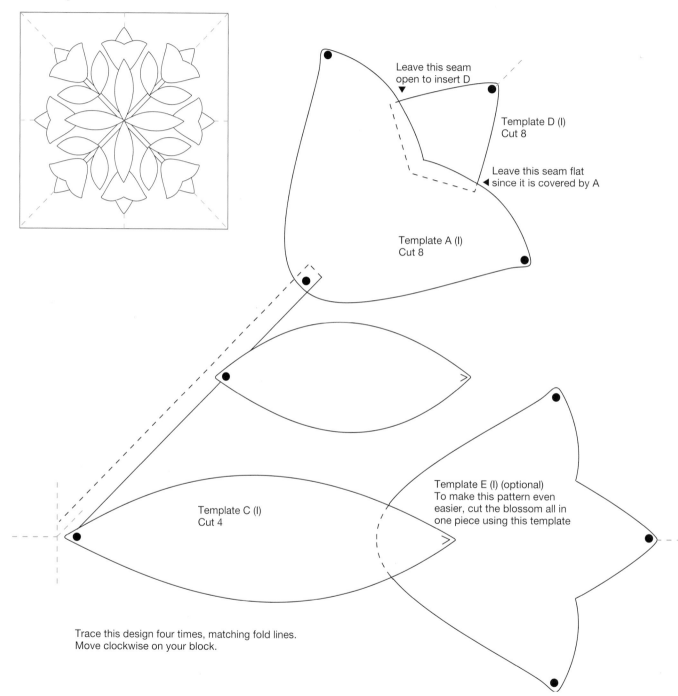

Leave this seam
open to insert D

Template D (I)
Cut 8

Leave this seam flat
since it is covered by A

Template A (I)
Cut 8

Template E (I) (optional)
To make this pattern even
easier, cut the blossom all in
one piece using this template

Template C (I)
Cut 4

Trace this design four times, matching fold lines.
Move clockwise on your block.

(like the end of a stem) are not turned under since they will be covered. In Version I, stems go down first, then the blossoms, then the leaves. (Understanding layering is mostly common sense. Just think through any pattern before you sew.) On this first layered pattern (only), dotted lines show where one piece lies under another. Let's walk through the layering process on Version I. Make the stems first.

Even More Unbelievable!

Today's Husqvarna Viking Designer I ESS is more exciting than ever. With 29 new features, your Husqvarna Viking Designer I ESS is one of the world's most advanced sewing and embroidery machines. New features, requested by you, are on our home page as updates for all Designer I owners to enjoy. That means your Designer I always has the latest innovations. The best part, all the exclusive patented features like the amazing Sensor System and Sewing Advisor™ make sewing truly incredible.

Visit our web site www.husqvarnaviking.com to find your nearest authorized Husqvarna Viking dealer.

Unique Internet updates. Exclusive features beyond compare.
The Husqvarna Viking Designer I ESS is even more unbelievable.

www.husqvarnaviking.com

Trumpeting Angel

by Jan Burns

Gold lamé adds a touch of elegance to this joyful little angel wall hanging. Try stitching another one with the motif reversed to make a matching pair!

MATERIALS

- ❏ 11″ x 19″ piece of dark green print fabric (for background)
- ❏ 8″ x 16″ piece of muslin or solid white fabric (for base)
- ❏ Metallic fabrics: 2″ x 6″ piece of light gold lamé, 3″ square of flesh-color lamé, 4″ x 8″ piece of medium gold lamé, 6″ x 14″ piece of gold brocade, 4″ x 8″ piece of pale yellow lamé (for appliqués)
- ❏ 1/8 yd. of gold lamé (for inner border)
- ❏ 1/2 yd. of holiday print fabric (for outer border and binding)
- ❏ 17″ x 25″ piece of backing fabric
- ❏ 17″ x 25″ piece of lightweight quilt batting
- ❏ Four 8″ x 16″ pieces of tear-away fabric stabilizer
- ❏ Two 12″ x 20″ pieces of paper-backed fusible web
- ❏ Metallic threads in colors to match metallic fabrics
- ❏ Rayon thread in flesh color to match flesh-color lamé
- ❏ Sewing thread in white and colors to match fabrics (for piecing)
- ❏ Clear nylon monofilament
- ❏ Non-stick pressing sheet
- ❏ Tracing paper
- ❏ Fabric chalk
- ❏ Basic sewing and pressing supplies

Skill level: Intermediate
Finished wall hanging size: 15″ x 23″

CUTTING DIRECTIONS

From the gold lamé, cut:
Two 1″ x 10 1/2″ strips and two 1″ x 18 1/2″ strips (for inner border)

From the holiday print fabric, cut:
Two 2 3/4″ x 10 1/2″ strips and two 2 3/4″ x 23 1/2″ strips (outer border)
Four 2″ x 25″ strips (for binding)

DIRECTIONS

Note: Use a 1/4″ seam allowance, unless otherwise indicated. Appliqué patterns are located in the pullout section and do not include a seam allowance.

1. Trace the appliqué shapes onto tracing paper. Indicate the right side in one corner of the pattern. Flip the tracing to the reverse side, then place the fusible web paper side up on the tracing. Trace each pattern piece separately onto the fusible web, leaving approximately 1/2″ between the pieces. Mark detail lines on each piece. Cut out 1/4″ beyond the marked lines.

2. Fuse the shapes onto the wrong side of the following appliqué fabrics (using a pressing sheet for the metallic fabrics): Piece A onto light gold lamé, Pieces B and C onto flesh-color lamé, Piece D onto medium gold lamé, Piece E onto gold brocade, and Piece F onto pale yellow lamé. Cut out

neatly. Place the design right side up on your work surface, then place the muslin on top and trace the design. Remove the paper backing from the appliqué shapes and, referring to the photograph, position them on the muslin in alphabetical order. Fuse the pieces onto the muslin. (**Note:** Do not move iron from side to side as shifting may occur.)

3. Place two sheets of fabric stabilizer beneath the muslin. With metallic or rayon thread in the top of the machine and white thread in the bobbin, use a narrow satin stitch for Pieces A, B, and C and a medium-width satin stitch for the other pieces. Working in alphabetical order, satin stitch over the inner detail lines on each piece. Set your machine for

straight stitch and use light gold metallic thread to work multiple rows of stitching on Piece F following the contours of the inner and outer detail lines and on Piece D following the inner detail lines only.

4. Remove the fabric stabilizer and fuse the web onto the back of the muslin (do not remove paper backing at this point). Carefully cut out the angel along the outer edges. Cut out area indicated by "X" on pattern. Remove paper backing and fuse angel onto center of green background. Place two sheets of fabric stabilizer under angel and, working in alphabetical order, satin stitch over any remaining inner edges and along all outer edges. Remove fabric stabilizer. Trim background to measure 10½" x 18½".

5. *Inner border.* Fold the 1" x 10½" gold lamé strips in half lengthwise with wrong sides facing and raw edges aligned. Pin each strip to the sides of the quilt center, right sides facing, aligning the raw edges. Sew using a ⅛" seam allowance. Stitch the 1" x 18½" strips to the top and bottom in the same manner.

6. *Outer border.* Sew the 2¾" x 10½" holiday print strips to the sides of the quilt top. Stitch the 2¾" x 23½" strips to the top and bottom of the quilt top in the same manner.

7. Layer the wall hanging top, batting, and backing. Baste the layers together. Set your machine for straight stitch. Using gold metallic thread, quilt close to the outer edges of the angel, close to the folded edges of the inner

border, and close to the outer border seam. Using white thread, quilt close to the outermost edge of the border. Using clear monofilament, quilt along all inner edges and satin-stitched design lines of the angel. Set your machine for free-motion quilting and use gold metallic thread to quilt a continuous line of meandering curves over the entire background (do not stitch over angel). Trim backing and batting even with wall hanging top.

8. Bind as desired with the 2" x 25" holiday print strips.

Jan Burns is a professional designer and past contributor to The Quilter *and the former editor of* Creative Quilting *magazine.* ❖

Poinsettia Table Runner

Set an exquisite holiday table with this beautiful table runner that is partially paper pieced!

by DeLoa Jones

Note: Yardage is based on 45" wide fabric by *Hoffman Fabrics*.

MATERIALS

❏ ¹/4 yd. of yellow print fabric
❏ ¹/3 yd. of red print fabric
❏ ¹/2 yd. of tan print fabric
❏ ¹/2 yd. of red and green snowflake print
❏ 1 yd. of dark green print fabric
❏ 1¹/2 yds. of backing fabric
❏ *YLI* clear monofilament
❏ *Superior Threads* in No. 205 Green Glitter and No. 201 Gold Glitter
❏ 21" x 49" piece of *Hobbs* Thermore batting
❏ *DeLoa's* Quick and Easy Printable Freezer Paper* (optional)
❏ Basic sewing and pressing supplies

Available through DeLoa's Quilt Shop at www.deloasquiltshop.com or call (616) 639-2123.

Skill level: Advanced
Finished block size: 10" x 10"
Number of blocks: 3
Finished runner size: 19" x 47"

CUTTING DIRECTIONS

Note: Cut all strips by the full width of the fabric. Patterns for Pieces C and D are located in the pullout section.

From the yellow print fabric, cut:
One 1¹/2" strip; crosscut into twenty-four 1¹/2" squares (for Unit A, Piece 2)
Three 1" strips (for inner border)

From the red print fabric, cut:
Two 4¹/2" strips; crosscut twenty-four 2¹/2" x 4¹/2" pieces (for Unit A, Piece 1)

From the tan print fabric, cut:
12 each of Pieces C and D (**Note:** Do not reverse these templates. Place the patterns on the *right* side of the fabric and cut.)
Two 3" strips; crosscut into forty-eight 1¹/2" x 3" pieces (for Unit B, Pieces 2 and 3)

From the red and green snowflake print fabric, cut:
One 15³/8" square; cut diagonally in half twice
Two 8" squares; cut diagonally in half once

From the dark green print fabric, cut:
Two 3" strips; crosscut into twenty-four 3" squares (for Unit B, Piece 1)
Four 2¹/2" wide strips (for outer border)
Seven 2¹/2" bias strips (for binding)

DIRECTIONS

Note: Use a ¹/4" seam allowance throughout. Paper piecing patterns are located in the pullout section. Seam allowances have been added around the outside of each unit.

Poinsettia Block Assembly

1. Using the paper piecing patterns provided, trace or copy on a copy machine 24 of Unit A and 24 of Unit B. To construct each Unit A, begin with a 2¹/2" x 4¹/2" red piece pinned right side up in the number 1 position on the unmarked side of the block. (**Note:** If using DeLoa's freezer paper,

trace the pattern on the paper side and fuse the material in place on the unmarked side instead of pinning.) Place a 1¹/2" yellow square right side down in the number 2 position making sure that the square extends at least ¹/4" beyond the marked area on all sides. Flip the unit over and sew on the marked line. Trim seam allowances to ¹/4", then trim along the outside pattern line of Unit A. (See **Diagrams 1** and **2**.)

fabric
freezer paper
Diagram 1   **Diagram 2**

2. For Unit B, begin with a 3" dark green square placed right side up in the number 1 position on the unmarked side of the block. Place a 1¹/2" x 3" tan piece right side down in the No. 2 and No. 3 positions and stitch in the same manner as step 1. Trim seam allowances to ¹/4", then trim along the outside pattern line of Unit B. (See **Diagrams 3** and **4**.)

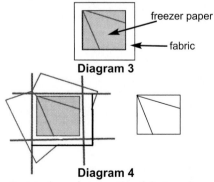

freezer paper
fabric
Diagram 3

Diagram 4

3. Mark a dot on the fabric where indicated on the paper patterns as a guide to stitching the inset seams. Remove the paper from the Unit A fabric pieces only.

PROJECT #4
**Pillow: "Dutch Bulbs a-Bloomin'
Version II."**
16" x 16".
Traditional pattern.

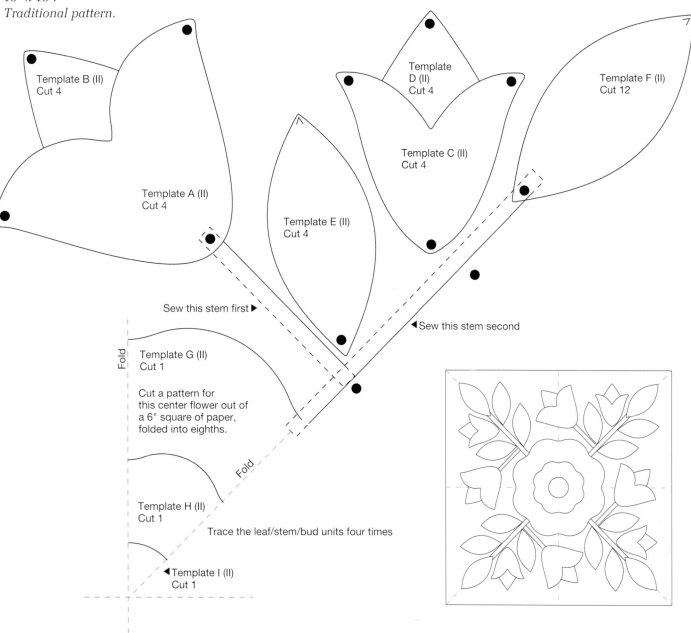

Template B (II)
Cut 4

Template D (II)
Cut 4

Template F (II)
Cut 12

Template A (II)
Cut 4

Template C (II)
Cut 4

Template E (II)
Cut 4

Sew this stem first ▶

◀ Sew this stem second

Fold

Template G (II)
Cut 1

Cut a pattern for
this center flower out of
a 6" square of paper,
folded into eighths.

Fold

Template H (II)
Cut 1

Trace the leaf/stem/bud units four times

◀ Template I (II)
Cut 1

METHOD #11: SUPERFINE STEMS

1. Fold the ¾" x 8½" strip of bias-cut green in half,
   lengthwise, right sides out.

2. Pin it to the background block. Pin it down its
   center so that the raw edges are on the dashed stem
   line marked on the block (Figure 3-1 B).

3. Sew the stem down with fine running stitches taken
   just to the raw edge side of the center (Figure 3-1 C).

These stitches will become the right-hand side of
the stem after you take the next step.

4. Fingerpress the folded side back up and over the
   raw edge side. Pin it in place, then appliqué it down
   (Figure 3-1 D). If any of the raw edge threatens to
   peek out from under, cut that underneath seam back a
   bit. Your first superfine stem is as easy as that!

Sometimes, as in Project #29, you will want a slightly
wider stem. Use 1" masking tape for this or cut a 1"-

PROJECT #5
Pillow: "Dutch Bulbs a-Bloomin' Version III."
16" x 16".
"Winding Rose," designed by Ellen Peters.

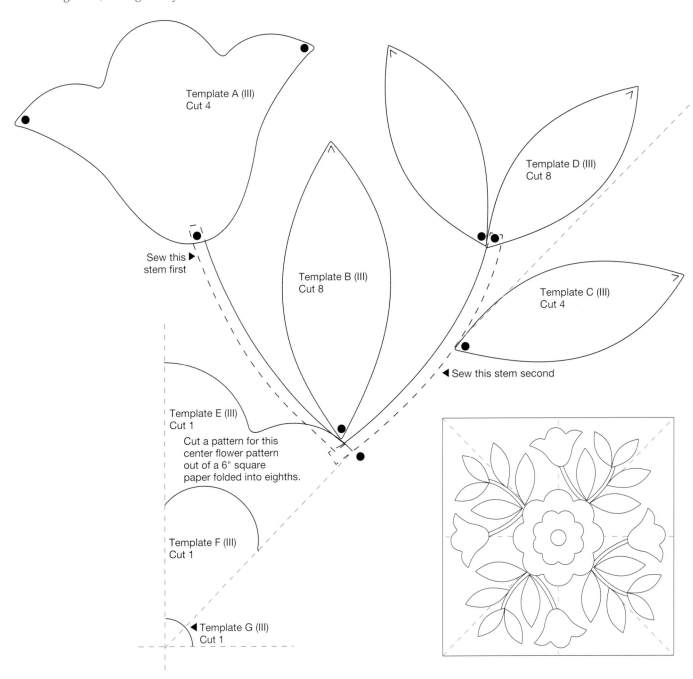

Template A (III)
Cut 4

Template D (III)
Cut 8

Template B (III)
Cut 8

Template C (III)
Cut 4

Sew this ▶
stem first

◀ Sew this stem second

Template E (III)
Cut 1

Cut a pattern for this
center flower pattern
out of a 6" square
paper folded into eighths.

Template F (III)
Cut 1

◀ Template G (III)
Cut 1

wide strip with a rotary cutter. On such a lengthy "stem" as the border stripes in Project #29, why not do the running stitches (Figure 3-1 C) by straight stitch on the sewing machine? There are also special bars available for making superfine stems from as narrow as ⅛" up to ½". Called Celtic Bias Bars™ or Bias Press Bars, they're sold in quilt shops.

Layered Flowers

1. When a smaller flower petal is layered underneath a larger flower base (templates A (I) and D (I)), sew the larger piece down to the background first.

2. Leave A's overlapping seam open, then slip the smaller piece (D) under it. To prepare template D, pin the freezer-paper template to the wrong side of

FIGURE 3-1 A-D.
Method #11: Superfine stems.

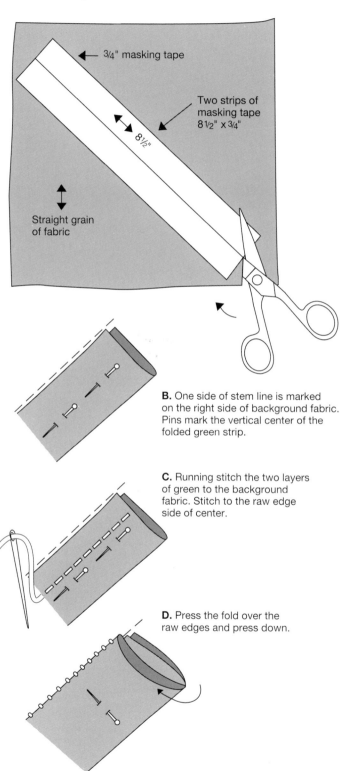

← 3/4" masking tape

Two strips of masking tape 8½" x ¾"

8½"

Straight grain of fabric

B. One side of stem line is marked on the right side of background fabric. Pins mark the vertical center of the folded green strip.

C. Running stitch the two layers of green to the background fabric. Stitch to the raw edge side of center.

D. Press the fold over the raw edges and press down.

FIGURE 3-2.
Layered flowers. When there are lots of layers to a flower, you may want to cut the background out from behind one or two of them. Here the background has been trimmed to ¼" from the seam of template I, and removed.

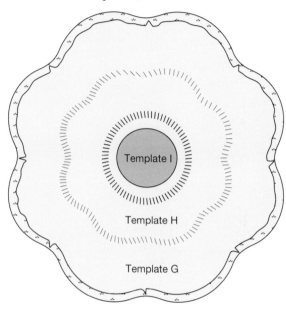

Template I

Template H

Template G

the fabric, then cut a ¼" seam around all sides of the template. Iron the two top-side seams up over the shiny surface of the freezer paper, but leave flat the seam that lies underneath A. Now appliqué template D's prepared seams.

3. Before sewing the seam that joins A and D, pull the freezer paper templates out of both units. Beyond layering, flowers can be made more dimensional with stuffed appliqué and folded fabric. If this appeals to you, leave A open, and read Method #13, which follows shortly. **Note:** The small pieces of a flower that are layered on top of a larger unit can be sewn onto the base of the flower before you appliqué the completed unit down to the back ground. Thus, for Version II, sew its center blossom from the top down, template I to H. Since there will be four layers of fabric, cut the back out of I, trimming the seam to ¼" from the seam line (Figure 3-2). On the flower base (G), pull out the freezer-paper template before you finish sewing the last petal. That leaves the background fabric uncut and for a pillow, it will be stronger. The flower's round center (template I) provides an opportunity to try Method #12.

METHOD #12: PERFECT GRAPES

You could make perfectly fine circles by any of our ten ways to appliqué, including Method #8. Needleturning a tight circle, however, is just plain slow going, so quiltmak-

FIGURE 3-3 A-B.
METHOD #12: Perfect grapes.

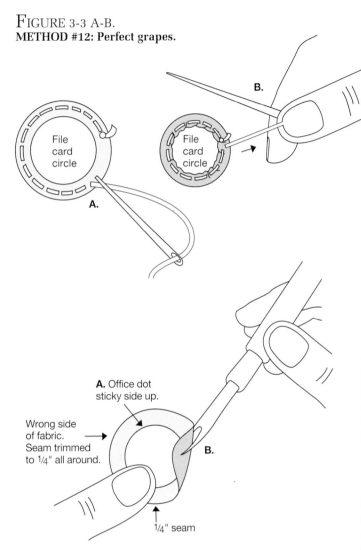

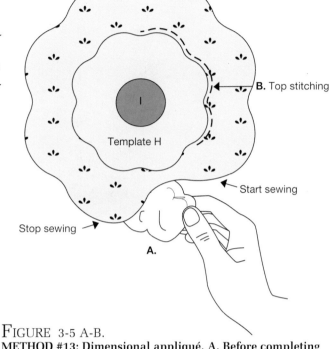

FIGURE 3-5 A-B.
METHOD #13: Dimensional appliqué. A. Before completing the flower's appliqué, push in a little polyester filling. B. Top stitching (same color thread) through the layers of the appliqué to the background fabric defines the shape and emphasizes its dimension.

FIGURE 3-4 A-B.
Office dot grapes.

ers have fine-tuned techniques for those precisely round circles. A favorite way is to make a file-card circle template the size of the finished grape: gather a circle of fabric over it, press the fabric, take the template out, and sew (Figure 3-3 A-B).

Perfect grapes can also be made with round color-coding labels (also called "office dots"). These circles come in three sizes: ¾" (just fits template G III), ½", and ¼". (They even come in grapelike ovals!) Office dots are great for holding a turned seam pressed to their sticky side. Here's how it's done. Stick an office dot to the wrong side of the fabric. Trim a ¼" seam around it. You could sew around this shape (as in Figure 3-3 A-B), fingerpress it, appliqué two-thirds of the way around the edge, then remove the dot before you finish sewing. Even faster, though, is this next step: Put the office dot on the wrong side of the

fabric with its sticky side facing you. Working flat on the table, push the cloth's edge up over the template. Use a seam ripper to press the seam to stick to the dot. Appliqué this perfect grape full circle. Then slit the background fabric underneath it and tweeze out the dot.

Perhaps you're thinking, "This technique sounds a bit far-out." That's exactly how I felt at the end of a long class in 1989, when a kind woman, whose name I no longer recall, pressed a sheet of office dots into my hand and said, "Here, try these." I'd like to thank her again, for those office dots have changed my life. All the grape patterns I've drawn since have ¾" and ½" grapes!

METHOD #13 [A BAKER'S DOZEN]: DIMENSIONAL APPLIQUÉ (WITH A FOLDED RIBBON FLOWER)

It's so easy to sew part way around an appliqué, push in a little polyester fiber-fil stuffing, then complete the sewing. Thus, "stuffed appliqué" is the most common form of dimensional appliqué. Try it on templates H and G on Version II or E and F on Version III (Figure 3-5 A). Top-stitching or quilting (echoing the appliqué's shape by ⅟₁₆") completes the effect (Figure 3-5 B). There's also dimensional appliqué that involves folding, gathering, or ruffling ("ruching") fabric. It is most often seen made into flowers. Let's try the simplest of fancy flowers, a folded ribbon

FIGURE 3-6 A-B.
Method #13:
Dimensional appliqué:
folded ribbon flower.
Begin with a 1½" x 4½"
rayon ribbon. Fold as
shown. Then stitch,
trim, gather,
tie off the
thread—and
there you have a
sweetheart of a
flower!

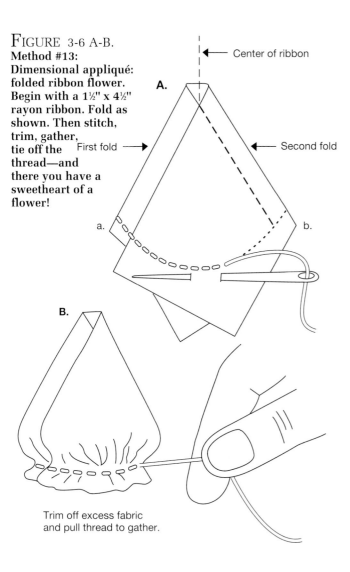

Trim off excess fabric
and pull thread to gather.

Needleturning the leaves

Mother Nature would not approve, but we have saved the leaves for last. Align leaf B's tip and base points with the tiny arrow (leaf tip) and bullet (leaf base) marked on your background fabric. With pins, match the pattern points on the appliqué to the pattern points marked on the background (Figure 3-7). Complete the pinning. If the pins bother you, baste with big stitches. Little pieces like leaves move out of alignment so easily, and the fix—big basting—takes only seconds. Do all leaf B shapes, then go on to the slightly trickier placement of leaf C. It is done the same way, using Method #4. With the flowers done by Method #8, you've given two very popular, but very different, appliqué methods a truly fair try. By now you have a sense of what works well for you. **Note:** Lisa Schiller suggests connecting the tip and base marks with a line following the vein of the leaf. This line would make a more complex block easier to follow, and being totally hidden by the leaf, it can't show.

FIGURE 3-7.

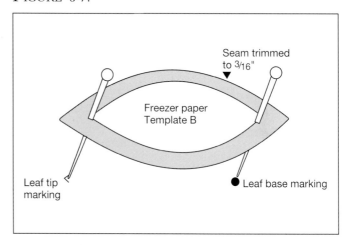

Preparing a leaf for Method #4: Needleturn appliqué.
Template B, cut from freezer paper, has been ironed on the
bias to the right side of the green fabric. The placement
markings from the pattern (an arrow for a leaf tip, a bullet
for a leaf base) are drawn on both the leaf and the back-
ground. Bring both sets of markings into alignment with pins
at the points. Secure (double pin or baste) the leaf to the
block and begin to needleturn. Peel off the freezer paper tem-
plate when the leaf is sewn. Since so little is marked on the
background, you can needleturn without concern for lining
up seams and drawn leaf shape with every stitch.

flower. Though rosebud-like, it works well on our "Dutch Bulbs a-Bloomin'." See it in the place of template D in Version I (and of D and B in Version II).

1. Fold a 4½" length of ribbon (1½" wide) as shown in Figure 3-6 A.

2. Sew the curved line with running stitches.

3. Pull the thread to gather. Keep the distance from point *a* to point *b* 1¼" long (Figure 3-6 B). Lock stitches and trim excess ribbon to an even seam.

4. Slip this bud (in place of template D) under the flower base's open edge (template A). Pull the freezer paper template out of A. Baste or pin the bud. Use two pins so the bud doesn't pivot out of position. Then sew it to just the top layer of the folded flower. Tack the top of the folded petal down to prevent "wilt," but leave its folds open.

CHAPTER 4

Fabric, Supplies, and Patterns

And now on to Chapter 4, for fabric specifications and the patterns and templates themselves, with brief assembly instructions. You can choose from quick projects, small quilts, and even bed-size quilts.

Re-read Chapter 2 for the materials and size seam needed for the appliqué method you select. How many of each pattern shape to cut is indicated on each template. Where there is more than one version of a pattern, the version number is given in parentheses, following the template letter. All patterns are given without seam allowance. Throughout, use the fabric section and the pattern section together to determine both fabric specifications and complete assembly instructions.

A great many of the patterns in this book use scraps. However, yardage amounts are given so that you can buy new cloth if necessary. The yardage estimate includes all the scraps in one given color group. Thus, seven squares 5" x 5", finished, made from red scraps will be listed as "assorted scraps or ¼ yard" for purchasing purposes. The smallest cut listed is ¼ yard, since that is generally the smallest yardage you can buy. All yardage is based on 45"-wide fabrics; stick to prewashed 100% cotton unless you are experienced in fabric selection for appliqué. Yardage estimations are based on the amount needed for the first appliqué method suggested for each project. Cutaway appliqué (Methods #1 and #2), for example, often uses more fabric than other methods (a fact well compensated for by its speed and ease). Estimations are modestly generous to allow for cutting errors, and to avoid piecing border strips more than once or backings more than twice. When economy is more important, rethink the yardage estimates and save. For ease of comprehension, fabric quantities are identified by the color used in the project's color photographs.

PROJECT #6
Apron (men's size): "Holly Wreathed Apron."
Fabric
- *Striped apron fabric:* 1¼ yards
- *Ribbon ties:* 67" of 1" grosgrain (19" for neck, 24" for each waist tie. Includes 1" hem.)
- *Green holly leaves:* assorted scraps, or ¼ yard green total
- *Red holly berries:* scrap or ¼ yard

PROJECT #7
Apron (women's size): "Lacy Heart Apron."
Fabric
- *Striped apron fabric:* 1 yard
- *Ribbon ties:* 79" of 1" grosgrain (23" for neck, 28" for each waist tie. Includes 1" hem.)
- *Red heart:* scrap or ¼ yard

PROJECT #8
Picture/House Blessing: "Welcome Home."
Fabric
- *For blue heart:* scrap or ¼ yard. For Method #1 or #2, cut a rectangle 9" x 12".
- *Neutral background fabric:* scrap or ½ yard. Cut a rectangle 12" x 15".

Other Supplies
- *Fusible web:* scrap or ¼ yard
- Black Pilot® SC-UF pen (see Chapter 2 for instructions for writing on cloth)
- Picture frame (8" x 10" [without mat] or 9" x 12" [with mat])

PROJECT #9
Picture/Token of Affection: "Friendship Is a Sheltering Tree."
Fabric
- *Rose color print:* scrap or ¼ yard. Cut one of template B; two of C and D. For variety, the birds can be made out of the reverse side of this fabric.
- *Moss green print:* scrap or ¼ yard. Cut one of template A.
- *Off-white background fabric:* scrap or ½ yard. Cut a rectangle 12" x 15".

Other Supplies
- *Fusible web:* scrap or ¼ yard
- Black or brown Pigma Micron® SDK pen in sizes .05 (for tracing the large calligraphy) and .01 for shading dots (see Chapter 2 for instructions for writing on cloth)
- Picture frame (9" x 12")

PROJECT #10
Picture: "Promises."
Fabric
- *Off-white background fabric:* ½ yard. Cut one square 18" x 18", finished. This allows sufficient fabric to accommodate framing.
- *Red print frame:* ½ yard. Cut one square 18" x 18", finished.
- *Figures (flesh, dress, shoes, hat, jacket, pants, dog):* scraps or ¼ yard each

Other Supplies
- Embroidery floss to embellish the figures
- Brown Pigma Micron SDK pen (.01) to draw features

PROJECT #11
Pillow: Patriotic Pillow I—"Peace, Love, and Liberty."
Fabric
- *Blue center square fabric:* ¼ yard. To get one square 8" x 8", finished, cut one square 8½" x 8½".
- *Natural stripes:* ¼ yard. To get four rectangles 1" x 8", finished, cut four 1½" x 8½" rectangles. To get 20 squares 1" x 1", finished, cut 20 squares 1½" x 1½" (template A plus ¼" seam allowance).
- *Red stripes:* ¼ yard. To get eight rectangles 1" x 8", finished, cut eight rectangles 1½" x 8½". To get 16 squares 1" x 1", finished, cut 16 squares 1½" x 1½".
- *Liberty Heart fabric:* Cut a 4¼" square of red, plus a 4¼" square of white (from ¼ yard), plus a 4¼" x 8" rectangle of blue (from ¼ yard), then piece together (see the Liberty Square piecing guide on the pattern) to make a patchwork square 8" x 8", finished.
- *Backing fabric:* ½ yard

Other Supplies
- 14" pillow form
- Embroidery thread: gold for stars, black for "Liberty" and the bird's eye

PROJECT #12
Pillow: Patriotic Pillow II—"Sweet Doves of Liberty."
Fabric
- *Red frame and heart wreath:* ½ yard. To get one square 14" x 14", finished, cut one square 14½" x 14½".
- *Natural background and doves:* ½ yard. To get one square 14" x 14", finished, cut one square 14½" x 14½". Cut two each of C and D.
- *Blue plaid for center:* scrap or ⅓ yard. To get one square 8¼" x 8¼", cut on the bias. Baste this square, centered on the 14½" x 14½" square of natural background fabric. Treat these two layered squares as one piece of background fabric.
- *Liberty Heart fabric:* Cut a 1¾" square of red, plus a 1¾" square of white, plus a 1¾" x 3" rectangle of blue, all cut from scrap pieces. Piece these together, following the Liberty Square piecing guide shown on the

pattern for Project #11. Using template E, cut the Liberty Heart appliqué from this patchwork square.

Other Supplies
- 14" pillow form
- Embroidery thread

PROJECT #13
Placemats: "Holly, Laurel, and Hearts Versions I and II."

Fabric (for two placemats)
- *Tan background fabric:* ½ yard. Cut two 12" x 18" rectangles.
- *Red heart and berry fabric:* scraps or ¼ yard. Cut two heart appliqués, adding seam allowance to the heart template. Cut 28 berries, adding seam allowance.
- *Leaf fabric:* scraps or ¼ yard. Cut 12 leaf appliqués, adding seam allowance.
- *Fusible web for Method #5:* ½ yard
- *Backing fabric:* ½ yard
- *Filler:* A soft thin terry towel works best inside the placemats, or use one crib/craft-size batt
- *Binding:* 62" per placemat (three packages [3 yards each] of doublefold binding will bind four placemats)

Other Supplies
- To personalize the mats, names can be hand embroidered using embroidery floss or machine satin stitching.
- Office dots (¾"), optional, for Method #12

PROJECT #14
Placemats: "Send Flowers! Versions I and II."

Fabric (for two placemats)
- *Blue background fabric:* ½ yard. Cut two 12" x 18" rectangles.
- *Blue/white fabric for vase:* scraps or ¼ yard. Cut two appliqués from the vase template, adding the seam allowance noted under the method selected.
- *Green fabric for leaves/stems:* scraps or ¼ yard. Cut six leaf appliqués, adding seam allowances to the leaf template shape. Cut four stems ¾" x 4", as in Method #11.
- *Red fabric for flowers:* scraps or ¼ yard. Cut six appliqués from template A, adding seam allowance.
- *Rose fabric for petals:* scraps or ¼ yard. Cut six rose petal appliqués from template B, adding seam allowance.
- *Rose ribbon for folded ribbon flowers:* 1 yard of 1½"-wide rayon French Wire Ribbon (or other ribbon). Each flower takes 4½" to make.
- *Blue ribbon for Version II's banner:* 14½" of 1½"-wide rayon
- *French Wire Ribbon (or other ribbon):* Clip out a "V" at each end. Seal the raw edge with Dritz® Fray Check™.
- *Backing fabric:* ½ yard

- *Filler:* A soft thin terry towel works best inside the placemats, or use one crib/craft-size batt
- *Binding:* 62" per placemat (three packages [3 yards each] of doublefold binding will bind four placemats)

PROJECT #15
Christmas tree skirt: "Katya's Angels."

Fabric
- *Green fabric for tree skirt:* 1⅓ yards. Cut a circle, 44" in diameter, finished. Cut a circle 5" in diameter, finished, out of the tree skirt's center.
- *Red fabric for angels and prairie point edging:* 1¾ yards. Cut about 100 squares, 3" x 3", for prairie points. Cut eight angel appliqués, adding the seam allowance noted under the method you choose.
- *Fusible web for Method #5:* ¾ yard
- *Backing fabric:* 1⅛ yard muslin
- *Batting:* One crib/craft-size batt
- *Binding:* Wide singlefold bias binding (two packages of 3 yards each)

PROJECT #16
Small quilt: "Heart of Country."

Fabric
- *Oyster white or natural fabric:* scraps or ⅓ yard. To get 31 white squares 3" x 3", finished, cut 31 squares 3½" x 3½".
- *Blue fabric #1 (Federal blue):* ⅔ yards
- *Blue fabric #2 (Prussian blue):* 1 yard (also used for borders). For center of quilt, cut squares from Federal blue and Prussian blue to make a total of 32 squares. To get 32 squares 3" x 3", finished, cut 32 squares 3½" x 3½".
  To get a top and bottom border, each 7½" x 21", finished, cut two rectangles 8" x 21½". To get two side borders, each 7½" x 27", finished, cut two rectangles 8" x 27½".
- *Blue fabric #3 (Williamsburg blue):* ⅓ yard. To get four blue border corner squares, each 7½" x 7½", finished, cut four squares 8" x 8".
- *Red/rose fabric for hearts:* assorted scraps or ⅔ yard. Cut 14 hearts from the heart template, adding the seam allowance noted under the method you choose.
- *Blue prairie points:* Use the leftovers from blues #1, #2, and #3. Cut 115 squares 3" x 3" to make prairie points. This allows some extras.
- *Backing fabric:* 1¼ yard
- *Batting:* One crib/craft-size batt

PROJECT #17
Small quilt: "Dutch Country Hearts Version I" (parent's quilt).

"Dutch Country Hearts Version II" (child's quilt).

Fabric (Version I: parent's quilt)
- *Beige background fabric:* assorted scraps or 1½ yards. To get 42 blocks 7" x 5½", finished, cut 42 rectangles 7½" x 6".
- *Red fabric for hearts:* assorted scraps or 1½ yards. For Method #1 or #2, cut 42 rectangles 7½" x 6" and mark each with a heart. For all other methods, cut 42 hearts on the bias, adding seam allowance all around.
- *Red print fabric for the inner border:* ⅓ yard. To get a top and bottom border, each 1" x 44", finished, cut two rectangles 1½" x 44½". To get two side borders, each 1" x 38½", finished, cut two rectangles 1½" x 39".
- *Khaki print fabric for the middle border:* ½ yards. To get a top and bottom border, each 2" x 48", finished, cut three rectangles 2½" x 44". Divide the third one in half to add the length needed to make two rectangles 2½" x 48½". To get two side borders, each 2" x 40½", finished, cut two rectangles 2½" x 41".
- *Red print fabric for the outer border:* 1¾ yards. To get a top and bottom border, each 5" x 58", finished, cut two rectangles 5½" x 58½", cutting along the selvage. To get two side borders, each 5" x 44½", finished, cut two rectangles 5½" x 45", cutting along the selvage.
- *Red print fabric for prairie points:* assorted scraps or 1 yard. Cut 150 squares 3" x 3", for prairie points. This allows some extras. Make the prairie point edging according to the directions in Project #16.
- *Backing fabric:* 3½ yards
- *Batting:* One full-size batt

Fabric (Version II: child's quilt)
- *Beige background fabric:* assorted scraps or ½ yard. To get 12 blocks 7" x 5½", finished, cut 12 rectangles 7½" x 6".
- *Red fabric for hearts:* assorted scraps or ½ yard. For Method #1 or #2, to get 12 hearts 7" x 5½", finished, cut 12 rectangles 7½" x 6". For all other methods, cut 12 hearts on the bias, adding seam allowance all around.
- *Red print fabric for the inner border:* ¼ yard. To get a top and bottom border, each 1" x 21", finished, cut two rectangles 1½" x 21½". To get two side borders, each 1" x 24", finished, cut two rectangles 1½" x 24½".
- *Khaki print fabric for the middle border:* ⅓ yard. To get a top and bottom border, each 2" x 23", finished, cut two rectangles 2½" x 23½". To get two side borders, each 2" x 28", finished, cut two rectangles 2½" x 28½".
- *Red print fabric for the outer border:* ½ yard. To get a top and bottom border, each 3" x 27", finished, cut two rectangles 3½" x 27½". To get two side borders, each 3" x 34", finished, cut two rectangles 3½" x 34½".
- *Red print fabric for prairie points:* assorted scraps or ⅔ yard. Cut about 100 squares 3" x 3", for prairie points. This allows some extras.
- *Backing fabric:* 1 yard
- *Batting:* One crib/craft-size batt

PROJECT #18
Small quilt: "Holly, Bows, and Berries."

Fabric
- *Tan solid fabric:* 1½ yards. To get four blocks 12" x 12" square, finished, cut four squares 12½" x 12½". To get four borders, each 6" x 36", finished, cut four rectangles 6½" x 40" (allows extra for miter).
- *Red fabric for bows and berries:* ⅓ yards. Cut four bows and 164 berries, adding seam allowance to each.
- *Green for leaves and stems:* 1 yard. Cut 156 leaves, adding seams. For border stems, cut seven ¾" x 44" strips for Method #11.
- *Backing fabric:* 1¼ yards
- *Batting:* One crib/craft-size batt
- *Binding:* 148"

PROJECT #19
Small quilt: "Mini-Sunbonnet Sue."

Fabric
- *Off-white background fabric:* 1 yard. To get nine 5" blocks, finished, cut nine 5½" x 5½" blocks. To get four borders, each 3" x 25", finished, cut four borders 3½" x 25½".
- *Blue fabric for border and sashings:* ¾ yard. To get four borders, each 3" x 25", finished, cut four borders 3½" x 25½". To get six horizontal sashing strips, each 1" x 5", finished, cut six sashing strips 1½" x 5½". To get four vertical sashing strips, each 1" x 17", finished, cut four vertical sashing strips 1½" x 17½". To get a top and bottom sashing strip, each 1" x 19", finished, cut two sashing strips 1½" x 19½".
- *Multicolors for Sunbonnet Sue:* scraps or ¼ yard each of various fabrics
- *Backing fabric:* 1 yard
- *Batting:* One crib/craft-size batt
- *Binding:* 104"

Other Supplies
- *Fusible web:* ½ yard

PROJECT #20
Small quilt: "Sugar Cookies."

Fabric
- *Off-white background fabric:* ¾ yards. To make 16 blocks 6" x 6", finished, cut 16 squares 6½" x 6½".
- *Teal fabric for border:* 1 yard. To make four borders, each 8" x 42", finished, cut four rectangles 8½" x 44" (allows extra for miter).
- *Large flower print fabric for feathers on border and inner border triangles:* 1¼ yard. To make four rectangles 8" x 42", finished, for the border appliqués, cut four rectangles 8½" x 44". To make 100 1" triangles, finished, cut 100 triangles the size of template C plus ¼" all around.
- *Burgundy print fabric for hearts and inner border triangles:* 1 yard. Cut and mark 16 blocks 6" x 6" for Method #1 or #2. For Method #8 (or #6, 7, 9, or 10), prepare 16 bias-cut hearts, adding seam allowance.

To make 100 triangles (each half of a 1" x 1" square, finished), cut 100 triangles the size of template C plus ¼" all around.
- *Backing fabric:* 2⅔ yards
- *Batting:* One twin-size batt
- *Binding:* 172"

PROJECT #21
Small quilt: "Honey Bee Hearts."

Fabric
- *Larger cran-raspberry print outer border fabric:* 1⅔ yards, cutting along selvage for length. To get a top and bottom border, each 5" x 45", finished, cut two rectangles 5½" x 45½". To get two side outer borders, each 5" x 55", finished, cut two rectangles 5½" x 55½". Cut one diamond appliqué, from template B, adding seam allowance.
- *Yellow solid inner border fabric:* ¼ yards. To get four inner borders, each 1½" x 42", finished, cut four rectangles 2" x 42½".
- *Smaller cran-raspberry print for corner squares:* ¼ yard. To get 20 corner squares 1½" x 1½", finished, cut 20 squares 2" x 2".
- *Olive stripe sashing strip fabric:* ½ yard. To get 24 sashing strips, each 1½" x 12", finished, cut 24 rectangles 2" x 12½".
- *Three beige/tan/brown print fabrics for "Honey Bee" background squares:* 1 yard, total. To get 108 template squares 3" x 3", finished, cut 108 squares 3½" x 3½".
- *Three shades of light raspberry print fabric to mix for the central squares of the Honey Bee Heart (template A) blocks:* ½ yard. To get nine squares 6" x 6", finished, cut nine squares 6½" x 6½".
- *Solid yellow fabric for one appliqué heart cut from template C:* 5½" x 5½" scrap
- *Two green print fabrics, for 108 appliqués cut from template D:* 1 yard
- *Brick red (plus scraps of two cran-raspberry print fabrics above) for the larger hearts:* ¼ yard. Cut four hearts from templates E and F, adding seam allowance.
- *Backing fabric:* 3¼ yards
- *Batting:* One full-size batt
- *Binding:* 224"

PROJECT #22
Small quilt: "Heartsong."

Fabric
- *Off-white background fabric:* 1 yard. To get a 30" x 30" square, finished, cut a 30½" x 30½" square.
- *Border print:* 1 yard. To get four borders, each 5" x 30", finished, cut four rectangles 5½" x 36" (allows extra for mitering). Sew the borders together, mitering the corners, before you appliqué them to the background square.
- *Bright red for hearts and flowers:* scraps or ¼ yard
- *Darker red for hearts and flowers:* scraps or ¼ yard

- *Lighter blue for bird's wings:* scrap or ¼ yard
- *Darker blue for bird's body:* scrap or ¼ yard
- *Green for leaves and stems:* ½ yard
- *Backing fabric:* 1 yard
- *Batting:* One crib/craft-size batt
- *Binding:* 124"

PROJECT #23
Small quilt: "Hearts and Crosses."

Fabric
- *Neutrals for squares and hands:* assorted scraps or ½ yard total. To get 31 background squares and 4 hands, 3½" x 3½", finished, cut 35 squares 4" x 4".
- *Red for corner squares and miniature hearts:* scraps or ¼ yard. For four red corner squares 3½" x 3½", finished, cut four squares 4" x 4".
- *Assorted colors:* scraps or ⅓ yard total. Cut 31 hearts from template A, adding ¼" seam allowance all around.
- *Assorted colors:* scraps or 2½ yards. Cut 272 of triangle template C, adding ¼" seam allowance all around. You need 68 sets of four triangles. A set is two of a dark color sewn opposite two of a bright color to form one 3½" x 3½" square, finished.
- *Border print:* To get a top and bottom border, each 3½" x 31½", finished, cut two rectangles 4" x 32". To get two side borders, each 3½" x 38½", finished, cut two rectangles 4" x 39".
- *Backing fabric:* 1½ yards
- *Batting:* One crib/craft-size batt
- *Binding:* 172"

PROJECT #24
Bed quilt: "Katya's Album."

Fabric
Blue fabric:
- Blue A (*appliquéd center*): ½ yards. To get two rectangles 14½" x 18", finished, cut two rectangles 15" x 18½".
- Blue B: 1¼ yard. To get one Border #1, 1" x 18", finished, cut one rectangle 1½" x 18½". To get two of Border #2, each 1" x 30" finished, cut two rectangles 1½" x 30½". To get two of Border #4, each 1" x 28" finished, cut two rectangles 1½" x 28½". To get two of Border #5, each 2" x 32" finished, cut two rectangles 2½" x 32½". To get two of Border #6, each 1" x 48" finished, cut three rectangles 1½" x 44". Piece together to get needed length for two rectangles 1½" x 48½". To get two of Border #7, each 1" x 42" finished, cut two rectangles 1½" x 42½". To get two of Border #10, each 2" x 62" finished, cut three rectangles 2½" x 44". Piece together to get needed length for two rectangles 2½" x 62½". To get two of Border #11, each 2" x 58" finished, cut three rectangles 2½" x 44". Piece together to get needed length for two rectangles 2½" x 58½".
- Blue C: ⅓ yard. To get two of Border #3, each 4" x 30" finished, cut two rectangles 4½" x 30½".

- *Blue D:* 1¾ yard or scraps. Cut 112 triangles the size of template D plus ¼" seam allowance all around. To get approximately 270 prairie points, cut 270 squares 3" x 3". See prairie point instructions in Project #16.
- *White fabric:* 2¼ yards. To get two center medallion rectangles 14½" x 18", finished, cut two rectangles 15" x 18½". To get 28 squares 4" x 4", finished, cut 28 squares 4½" x 4½". To get 28 squares from template C, cut 28 squares the size of template C plus ¼" seam allowance all around. To get two of Border #8, each 6" x 50" finished, cut three border pieces 6½" x 44". Piece together to get needed length for two rectangles 6½" x 50½".To get two of Border #9, each 6" x 54" finished, cut three border pieces 6½" x 44". Piece together to get needed length for two rectangles 6½" x 54½".
- *Backing fabric:* 4 yards (use some in squares and prairie points)
- *Batting:* One twin-size batt

PROJECT #25
Bed quilt: "Hearts and Flowers Border Quilt."

Fabric

- *White background fabric:* 5½ yards. (To save fabric, cut the borders first, and then the blocks. Fabric specifications are listed in optimum order of cutting.) To get a top and bottom border, each 8" x 52", finished, cut two rectangles 8½" x 52½". To get two side borders, each 8" x 85", finished, cut two rectangles 8½" x 85½". To get 12 appliqué blocks 16" x 16", finished, cut 12 squares 16½" x 16½", cutting along selvage for needed length.
- *Blue print fabric:* 6 yards. (To save fabric, cut the borders and horizontal sashing strips first, and then the blocks and the vertical sashing strips. Fabric specifications are listed in optimum order of cutting.) For appliqués (Method #2 or #1) for top and bottom border, each 8" x 52", finished, cut two rectangles 8½" x 52½", cutting along selvage for needed length. For appliqués (Method #2 or #1) for side borders, each 8" x 85", finished, cut two rectangles 8½" x 85½", cutting along selvage for needed length. To get nine horizontal sashing strips, each 1" x 16", finished, cut nine rectangles 1½" x 16½". To get two horizontal sashing strips, each 1" x 52", finished, cut two rectangles 1½" x 52½". To get 12 appliqué blocks 16" x 16", finished, cut 12 squares 16½" x 16½". To get four vertical sashing strips, each 1" x 67", finished, cut four rectangles 1½" x 67½".
- *Backing fabric:* 5 yards
- *Batting:* One full-size batt
- *Binding:* 310"

PROJECT #26
Bed quilt: "Oak Leaves and Reel."

Fabric

- *White or off-white background fabric:* 5 yards. To get 20 appliqué blocks 16" x 16", finished, cut 20 squares 16½" x 16½".
- *Print fabric for six blocks made with leaf template A:* 1½ yards. To get six appliqué blocks 16" x 16", finished (by Method #2 or #1), cut six squares 16½" x 16½".
- *Print fabric for six blocks made with leaf template B:* 1½ yards. To get six appliqué blocks 16" x 16", finished (by Method #2 or #1), cut six squares 16½" x 16½".
- *Print fabric for eight blocks made with leaf template C:* 2 yards. To get eight appliqué blocks 16" x 16", finished (by Method #2 or #1), cut eight squares 16½" x 16½".
- *Striped fabric for sashing strips:* 2½ yards. To get two vertical sashing strips, each 2" x 88", finished, cut two rectangles 2½" x 88½", cutting along selvage to get needed length. To get 16 horizontal sashing strips, each 2" x 16", finished, cut 16 rectangles 2½" x 16½", cutting along selvage.
- *Border print:* 3 yards. To get a top and bottom border, each 7½" x 70", finished, cut two rectangles 8" x 70½", cutting along selvage for needed length. To get two side borders, each 7½" x 103", finished, cut two rectangles 8" x 103½", cutting along selvage.
- *Backing fabric:* 6 yards
- *Batting:* One king-size batt
- *Binding:* 380"

PROJECT #27
Bed quilt: "Beribboned Irish Chain."

Fabric

- *Green print for borders:* 2⅔ yards. For a bottom border, 9" x 64", finished, cut one rectangle 9½" x 64½", cutting along selvage for needed length. For two side borders, each 9½" x 94½", finished, cut two rectangles 9½" x 94½", cutting along selvage for needed length.
- *Assorted greens for blocks:* scraps or 1⅔ yards. To get 240 squares 2½" x 2½", finished, cut 240 squares 3" x 3".
- *Red fabric for setting blocks and border appliqués:* 5 yards. To get border appliqués (22 bows, 19 full swags, 2 half-swags, and 2 corner swags) by Method #2 or #1, cut one bottom border rectangle 9½" x 64½", cutting along selvage for needed length. Cut two side border rectangles 9½" x 94½". Mark the appliqué shapes on these rectangles and pin them to the green borders. To get 35 plain setting blocks 7½" x 7½", finished, cut 35 blocks 8" x 8". To get 24 half-square triangles for edging, cut 12 blocks 8⅜" x 8⅜", then cut in half on the diagonal. To get four one-quarter-square triangles for corners, cut one 8¾" x 8¾" square. Cut into quarters on the diagonal.
- *Backing fabric:* 6 yards
- *Batting:* One queen-size batt
- *Binding:* 356"

PROJECT #28
Bed quilt: "Star of Hearts."

Fabric

- *Off-white background fabric:* 5¾ yards. To get 32 blocks 10" x 10" square, finished, cut 32 blocks 10½" x 10½". To get 16 half-square triangles for edging, cut eight blocks 10⅞" x 10⅞". Cut in half on the diagonal. To get two quarter-square triangles for corners, cut one 11¼" x 11¼" square. Cut in quarters on the diagonal. To get 81 sashing strips 2½" x 10", finished, cut 81 rectangles 3" x 10½". To get 32 sashing corner squares 2½" x 2½", finished, cut 32 squares 3" x 3". To get 16 half-square triangles (to complete the sashing strips where they meet the quilt's edges), cut eight blocks 3⅜" x 3⅜". Cut in half on the diagonal. To get two quarter-square triangles (to complete the upper left and lower right sashing strips where they meet the quilt's outer corners), cut one 2½" x 2½" square. Cut in quarters on the diagonal.

- *Red fabric for stars, hearts, and border squares and diamonds:* assorted (8-10) red calico scraps or 3¾ yards red calico. To get 32 red star appliqués, cut and mark template A stars on 32 squares 10" x 10". To get 48 red heart appliqués, cut the 32 hearts out of the center of the stars. (The hearts on the star blocks are reverse appliquéd by Method #3, to reveal the off-white background underneath.) In addition, use heart template B to cut 16 more hearts. Template B includes the ⅛" seam allowance. Cut 16 squares the shape of template C, adding a ⅛" appliqué seam allowance all around. Cut 64 diamonds the shape of template D, adding ⅛" appliqué seam allowance all around. Cut the two upper right and lower left corner appliqués (templates E and F).

- *Backing fabric:* 5 yards
- *Batting:* One queen-size batt
- *Binding:* 320"

PROJECT #29
Bed quilt: "Twining Blooms and Baskets."

Fabric

- *Background:* 2 yards (you'll use this same fabric for both the blocks and the flower centers). To get 20 blocks 9" x 9", finished, cut 20 blocks 9½" x 9½". Cut 26 flower centers using template #8, and 22 using template #11.

- *Tan solid for basket blocks and borders:* 3 yards. (To save fabric, cut the borders first, and then the blocks. Fabric specifications are listed in optimum order of cutting.) To get a top and bottom border, each 8" x 59", finished, cut two rectangles 8½" x 59½", cutting along selvage for needed length. To get two side borders, each 8" x 71¾", finished, cut two rectangles 8½" x 72¼", cutting along selvage. Cut 20 basket block appliqués, 9" x 9", cutting along selvage. (Fold 9" square freezer paper into fourths, trace the basket pattern onto it, then cut all four layers. Iron this pattern onto a 9" solid tan block, then proceed by Method #2.)

- *Navy print:* 2½ yards To get 12 setting blocks 9" x 9", finished, cut 12 squares 9½" x 9½". To get 14 half-square triangles for edging, cut 7 blocks 9⅞" x 9⅞". Cut in half on the diagonal. To get four quarter-square triangles for corners, cut one 10¼" x 10¼" square. Cut in half on the diagonal. Cut flower piece #10 from this print also. To get four border stripes, each ¼" x 59", finished, cut six strips 1" x 44", and piece to get needed length for stripes 1" x 59½". To get four border stripes, ¼" x 71¾", finished, cut eight strips 1" x 44", and piece to get needed length for stripes 1" x 72¼". You may wish to cut these a little longer for leeway. Use Method #11 to do the border stripes which measure ¼" wide, finished.

- *Maroon print:* 1¼ yards. To get four top and bottom border edging stripes, each ¼" x 58", finished, cut six strips 1" x 44", and piece for needed length for stripes 1" x 59½". To get four border stripes, each ¼" x 58", finished, cut eight strips 1" x 44", and piece for needed length for stripes 1" x 72¼".
Cut 26 flower piece appliqués from template #7, and 22 from template #12.

- *Green print:* 2 yards. For vine by Method #2 or #1, cut two strips 6½" x 60", and two strips 6½" x 72", cutting along selvage for length.
- *Backing fabric:* 5 yards
- *Batting:* One queen-size batt
- *Binding:* 298"

The Color Section

1

2

3

¹PROJECT #1
Small Quilt: You've Stolen My Heart!
25" x 30". Designed and made by the author.

²PROJECT #2
Small Quilt: Be My Valentine
25" x 30". Designed and made by Libby Hamilton Samuel.

³PROJECTS #3 and #4
Pillows: Dutch Bulbs a-Bloomin' Versions I and II
Made by Ellen Peters who also made the pillows shown
on the back cover (Project #5, Version III).

4

5

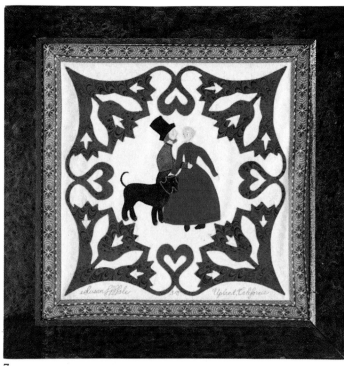

7

6

⁴PROJECTS #6 and #7
Aprons: Holly Wreathed Apron and Lacy Heart Apron
Holly Wreath Apron designed and made by Irene
Barker; Lacy Heart Apron designed and made by Mary
Sue Thomas Hannan.

⁵PROJECT #8
Picture/House Blessing: Welcome Home
The third picture uses Project #8's pattern, but with an
inscription for Sue and Tom Hannan's fiftieth wedding
anniversary. Designed and made by the author.

⁶PROJECT #9
Picture/Token of Affection: Friendship Is a
Sheltering Tree
Designed and made by the author for Emily and
Walter Filling.

⁷PROJECT #10
Picture: Promises
The block, framed here, is also ideal for an Album
Quilt. Appliquéd and embroidered by Sue Hale.
Designed by the author, incorporating figures from an
antique quilt.

8

10

9

11

⁸PROJECT #11
Patriotic Pillow I: Peace, Love, and Liberty
Designed and made by Faye Labanaris.

⁹PROJECT #12
Patriotic Pillow II: Sweet Doves of Liberty
Designed and made by Faye Labanaris.

¹⁰PROJECTS #13 and #14
Placemats: Holly, Laurel, and Hearts Versions
I and II, and Send Flowers! Versions I and II
Designed by the author; sewn by Carol Elliott.

¹¹PROJECT #15
Christmas Tree Skirt: Katya's Angels
45¹/₂" diameter. Designed by the author. Sewn by the author
and Carol Elliott; quilted by Joyce Hill.

12

13

14

¹²PROJECT #16
Small Quilt: Heart of Country
37¹/₂" x 43¹/₂". Designed, inscribed, and sewn by the author; quilted by Joyce Hill.

¹³PROJECT #17
Small Quilts: Dutch Country Hearts, Version I (left)
59¹/₂" x 56".
Dutch Country Hearts, Version II (right)
35¹/₂" x 34¹/₂". Designed by the author. Machine sewn by the author and Carol Elliott; quilted by Joyce Hill.

¹⁴PROJECT #18
Small Quilt: Holly, Bows, and Berries
50" x 50". The pattern is for a slightly smaller quilt (36" x 36").
Designed and made by Jeannie Koch.

¹⁵PROJECT #19
Small Quilt: Mini-Sunbonnet Sue
25" x 25". Designed and made by Suzanne (Sue) W. Linker.

15

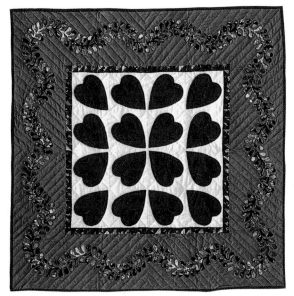

16

18

16PROJECT #20
Small Quilt: Sugar Cookies Version I
42" x 42". Pattern designed by the author;
made by Julee Prose.

18PROJECT #20
Small Quilt: Sugar Cookies Version III
42" x 42". A reverse appliqué version of Project
#20, made by Eva Wampler. Eva has reverse
appliquéd a red print heart with a leaf cutout,
down to a solid red heart.

17

17PROJECT #20
Small Quilt: Sugar Cookies Version II
45" x 45". A scrap quilt version of Project #20.
Made by Marilyn Allender.

19PROJECT #21
Small Quilt: Honey Bee Hearts
55" x 55". Machine pieced, appliquéd, and
quilted by Jeanne Elliott. Pattern and fabric
design by the author.

19

20

22

21

23

20PROJECT #22
Small Quilt: Heartsong
30" x 30". Designed and sewn by Suzanne (Sue) W. Linker
for whom it serves as a teaching quilt.

21PROJECT #23
Small Quilt: Hearts and Crosses
$38^1/_2$" x $45^1/_2$". Made by Katherine Kent Iverson Fowle.

22PROJECT #25
Bed Quilt: Hearts and Flowers Border Quilt
$76^1/_2$" x $93^1/_2$". New York, circa 1860. The pattern is for a
smaller quilt (68" x 85"). (Purchase, Mrs. Roger Brunschwig
Gift, 1988. Accession #1988.24.2. Photo courtesy of
Metropolitan Museum of Art.)

24

²³PROJECT #26
Bed Quilt: Oak Leaves and Reel
89¹/₂" x 109". The pattern is for a slightly smaller quilt
(85" x 103"). (Accession #10-124. Photo courtesy of
Shelburne Museum, Shelburne, Vermont.)

²⁴PROJECT #24
Small Quilt: Katya's Album
59¹/₂" x 67¹/₂". This birthday quilt was made to
remember young Katya Sienkiewicz's school friends
and neighbors. Designed and hand blanket stitched by
the author. Machine pieced by Audrey Waite; edged by
Mary Sue Hannan; quilted by Mona Cumberledge.

25

27

26

25PROJECT #27
Bed Quilt: Beribboned Irish Chain
82" x 94". Designed and made by Mary Sue
Thomas Hannan.

26PROJECT #28
Bed Quilt: Star of Hearts
79" x 79". Appliqué quilt inscribed, in part,
"Mrs. Eliza Palmer, June 2, 185[?]." From
Binghamton, New York. In the author's family.

27PROJECT #29
Bed Quilt: Twining Blooms and Baskets
67$\frac{1}{2}$" x 79$\frac{3}{4}$". Quilt pattern designed by the author
(no pattern is included for the pillow). Made by
Judy Sabbag.

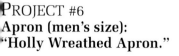

PROJECT #6
**Apron (men's size):
"Holly Wreathed Apron."**

Designed by Irene Barker.

PROJECT #7
**Apron (women's size):
"Lacy Heart Apron."**

Designed by Sue Hannan.

Hand Appliqué Method(s):
For heart: #5, 4, or 2
(also #1, 6, 7, 8, 9, or 10).
For wreath: #8, 5, 4, or 2
(also #1, 6, 7, 9, or 10).

Appliqué Ease Level: Super Easy!

Assembly
Make apron. On man's apron, the appliqué has to be done last. On the woman's, hem the pocket but appliqué the heart on before sewing the pocket to the apron. Instructions are on the pattern.

For the holly wreath: appliqué the 14 holly leaves over a 7½" circle drawn on the bib.

To make the berries: turn the outside edge under ⅛" and hem this to the circle with running stitches. Pull the sewing thread to gather slightly. Insert a bit of stuffing, rolled to the size of a plump pea. Draw the gathering thread tight. Backstitch to lock the thread, then continue on with this same thread to tack the berry firmly to the wreath.

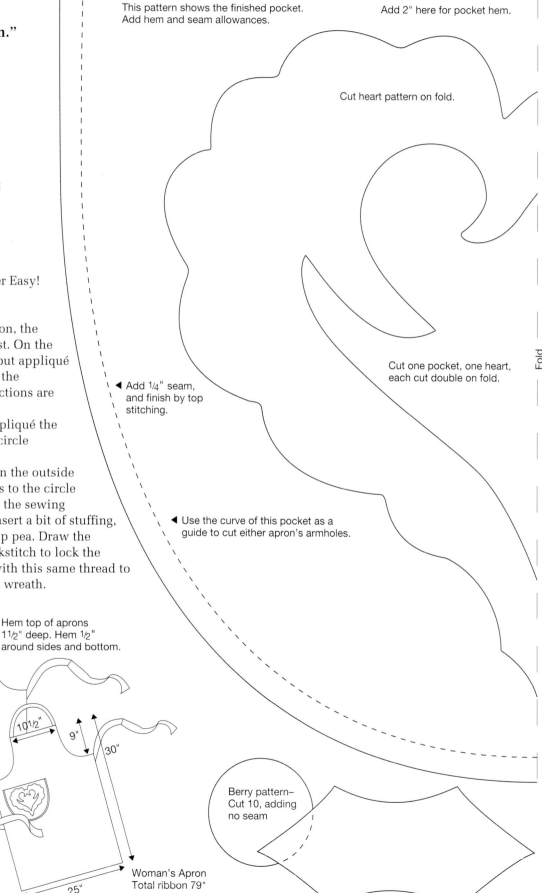

This pattern shows the finished pocket. Add hem and seam allowances.

Add 2" here for pocket hem.

Cut heart pattern on fold.

◄ Add ¼" seam, and finish by top stitching.

Cut one pocket, one heart, each cut double on fold.

Fold

◄ Use the curve of this pocket as a guide to cut either apron's armholes.

Hem top of aprons 1½" deep. Hem ½" around sides and bottom.

121½"

39½" | 10"

10½"

9"

30"

39⅜"

Man's Apron
Total ribbon 67"

25"

Woman's Apron
Total ribbon 79"

Berry pattern—
Cut 10, adding
no seam

PROJECT #8
**Picture/House Blessing:
"Welcome Home."**

9" x 12."
Designed by the author.

Hand Appliqué Method(s):
#5 or #1, 2, or 4.

Appliqué Ease Level:
Super Easy! by Method
#5. Moderately Easy,
but faster, by the others.

Assembly
Appliqué the heart. Trace the
inscription. Mount the picture
in a ready-made frame.

NOTE: *To fabric cover
an optional mat for
the picture, cut a
rectangle of fabric
1" bigger than the
mat's outside
dimensions. Put a
dab of glue (use a
gluestick) on the
two long sides of
the mat, then press
this glued surface,
centered, to the
wrong side of the
fabric. Rub the
gluestick down the mat's
two long sides, covering
a ½"-wide strip along the
mat's outer edges.
Fingerpress the fabric to
this, then iron the glue
dry. Do the same across
the two remaining sides
of the mat. Next, trim
the fabric back to 1"
parallel to the mat
opening, all around. To
miter the seam, cut on
the diagonal up to 1/16"
from the mat's inside
corners. Now glue (and
iron dry) the cloth to the
back of the mat's
window opening.*

Welcome Home

Fold

PROJECT #9
Picture/Token of Affection: "Friendship Is a Sheltering Tree."

9" x 12".
Designed by the author.

Hand Appliqué Method(s): #5.

Appliqué Ease Level: Easy

Assembly
Trace templates A and B (with B as one separate piece to lie under A) onto the fusible web. Prepare as described in Method #5. Iron B down to the background, then A. Blanket stitch template B's inside edge (for decoration only). Cut and apply the birds (templates C and D). Trace the inscription and the top and bottom banners. Lots of tiny dots shade the piece and are thicker nearest the appliqué shapes. Mount in a frame.

Template D
Cut 2

Template C
Cut 2

*Friendship is
A Sheltering Tree*

◀ Template B

◀ Template A

◀ Blanket stitch

Template B ▶

Fold

PROJECT #10
Picture: "Promises."

15" x 15" (including striped border. The red paper-cut framed album block itself is 12½" x 12½", finished.)
Pattern designed by the author, incorporating figures from an antique quilt.

Hand Appliqué Method(s): #5 for the paper-cut frame, #4 for the figures.

Appliqué Ease Level: Moderately easy for the paper-cut frame, using Method #5; with Method #1 or #2, it's A Challenge.

Assembly
To make a complete paper-cut frame pattern, trace template A onto a 12½" x 12½" square of paper folded into eighths. Match fold lines. Iron the same fold lines into the background fabric for placing the figures. Appliqué the frame (A) first, then the figures. Embellish the figures with embroidery and ink as desired. To stretch and frame the picture, take it to a do-it-yourself framing shop. For a faux grain finish like the model, use an antiquing kit.

Frame: Template A
⅛" of a square border,
12½" x 12½" finished

Diagonal center line

Fold

Fold   Horizontal center line

Horizontal center line

Vertical center line
for figures

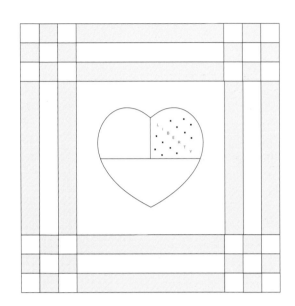

PROJECT #11
**Pillow: Patriotic Pillow I—
"Peace, Love, and Liberty."**

14" x 14".
Designed by Faye Labanaris.

Hand Appliqué Method(s): #4, #6, or #7.

Appliqué Ease Level: Super Easy!

Assembly
Piece the Liberty Square, then trace template B onto it, adding the ¼" seam allowance when cutting. Appliqué the Liberty Heart to the blue center square. Make nine-patch corners (template A) and four sets of border stripes. Attach to each side of the blue square. Embroider. Quilt if you choose, and complete into a pillow.

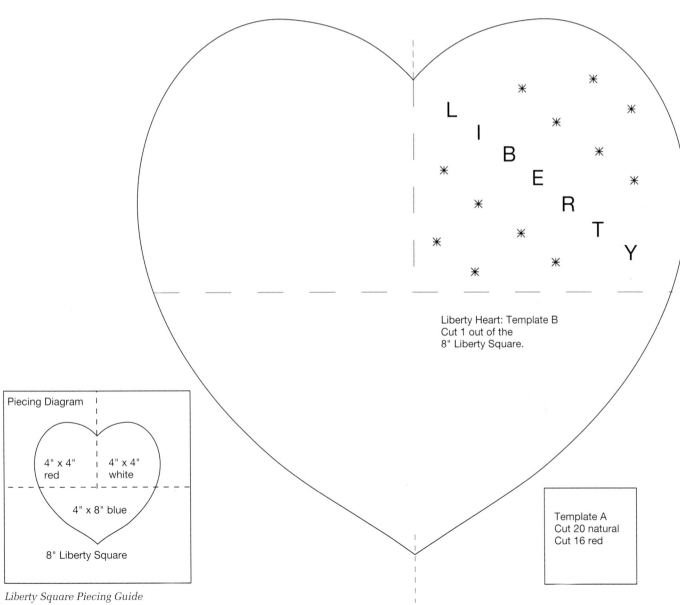

Liberty Heart: Template B
Cut 1 out of the
8" Liberty Square.

Piecing Diagram

4" x 4" red | 4" x 4" white

4" x 8" blue

8" Liberty Square

Template A
Cut 20 natural
Cut 16 red

Liberty Square Piecing Guide

PROJECT #12
Pillow: Patriotic Pillow II—
"Sweet Doves of Liberty."

14" x 14".
Designed by Faye Labanaris.

Hand Appliqué Method(s):
For red frame and heart wreath, Method #2 (using "pattern bridges" as noted on the pattern). For doves, Method #4 or #8. For Liberty Heart, Method #4.

Appliqué Ease Level: Easy

Assembly
Appliqué the red frame (template A) and the heart wreath (template B) as one bridged pattern using Method #2. Begin sewing inside the wreath. When that is sewn, trim the outside of the heart wreath to ³⁄₁₆" seam allowance. (Pin the red frame a bit more since it is now cut loose.) Lift the outside of the wreath to trim the blue plaid center square so that the heart wreath covers it completely. Now sew the wreath's outside edge. Sew the red frame, the doves, and the Liberty Heart. Embroider. Quilt if you choose, and complete into a pillow.

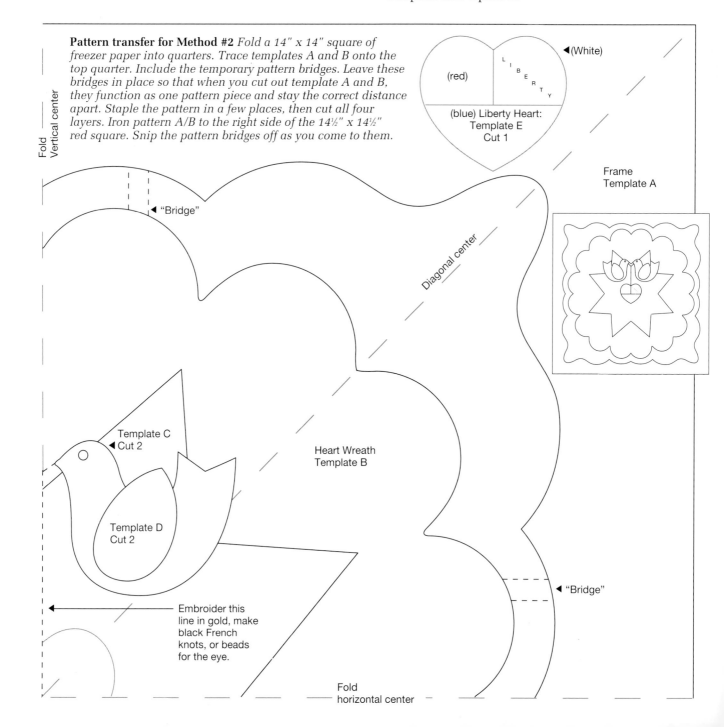

Pattern transfer for Method #2 *Fold a 14" x 14" square of freezer paper into quarters. Trace templates A and B onto the top quarter. Include the temporary pattern bridges. Leave these bridges in place so that when you cut out template A and B, they function as one pattern piece and stay the correct distance apart. Staple the pattern in a few places, then cut all four layers. Iron pattern A/B to the right side of the 14½" x 14½" red square. Snip the pattern bridges off as you come to them.*

Fold Vertical center

(red)   LIBERTY   ◀ (White)
(blue) Liberty Heart:
Template E
Cut 1

Frame
Template A

◀ "Bridge"

Diagonal center

Template C
◀ Cut 2

Heart Wreath
Template B

Template D
Cut 2

◀ "Bridge"

Embroider this line in gold, make black French knots, or beads for the eye.

Fold
horizontal center

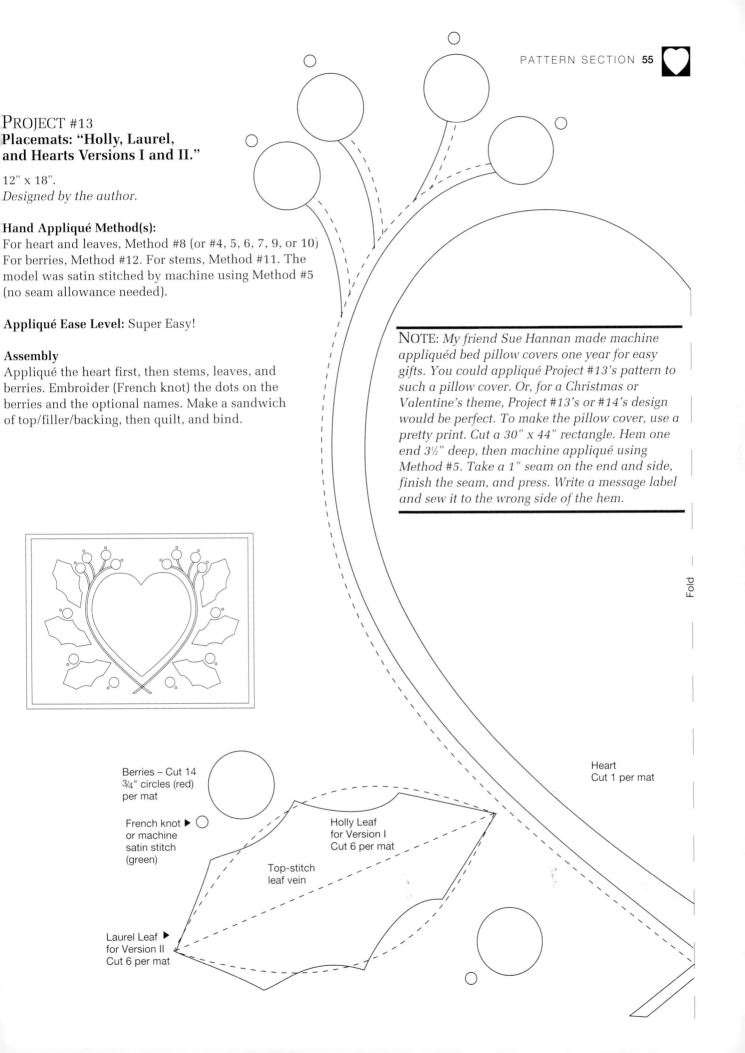

PROJECT #13
Placemats: "Holly, Laurel, and Hearts Versions I and II."

12" x 18".
Designed by the author.

Hand Appliqué Method(s):
For heart and leaves, Method #8 (or #4, 5, 6, 7, 9, or 10) For berries, Method #12. For stems, Method #11. The model was satin stitched by machine using Method #5 (no seam allowance needed).

Appliqué Ease Level: Super Easy!

Assembly
Appliqué the heart first, then stems, leaves, and berries. Embroider (French knot) the dots on the berries and the optional names. Make a sandwich of top/filler/backing, then quilt, and bind.

NOTE: *My friend Sue Hannan made machine appliquéd bed pillow covers one year for easy gifts. You could appliqué Project #13's pattern to such a pillow cover. Or, for a Christmas or Valentine's theme, Project #13's or #14's design would be perfect. To make the pillow cover, use a pretty print. Cut a 30" x 44" rectangle. Hem one end 3½" deep, then machine appliqué using Method #5. Take a 1" seam on the end and side, finish the seam, and press. Write a message label and sew it to the wrong side of the hem.*

Fold

Berries – Cut 14
3/4" circles (red)
per mat

French knot ▶
or machine
satin stitch
(green)

Holly Leaf
for Version I
Cut 6 per mat

Top-stitch
leaf vein

Laurel Leaf ▶
for Version II
Cut 6 per mat

Heart
Cut 1 per mat

PROJECT #14
**Placemats: "Send Flowers!
Versions I and II."**

12" x 18".
Designed by the author.

Hand Appliqué Method(s):
For vase, leaves, and flowers, use Method #8 (or #4, 5, 6, 7, 9, or 10). For folded ribbon flowers, use Method #13. For stems, Method #11. The model was satin stitched by machine using Method #5.

Appliqué Ease Level: Super Easy!

Assembly
Appliqué stems, flowers, leaves, and vase. For Version II's message banner, trace "Happy Birthday" (or any message) onto the 14½" ribbon. (See Chapter 2 for how to write on fabric.) Fold the banner, glue it lightly in place, then tack stitch or machine zigzag edge with invisible nylon thread. Make a sandwich of top/filler/backing; quilt, and bind.

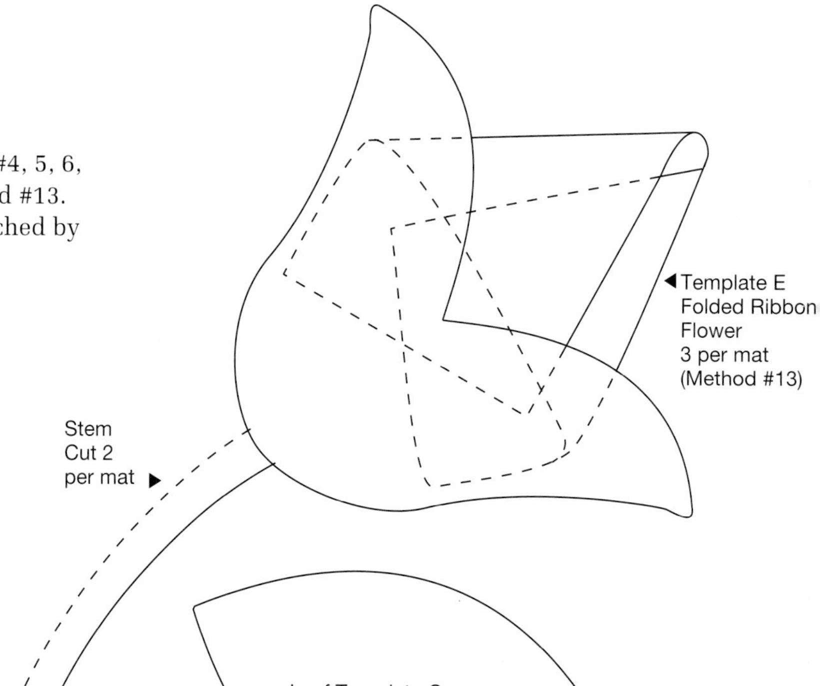

Template E
Folded Ribbon
Flower
3 per mat
(Method #13)

Stem
Cut 2
per mat ▶

Leaf Template C
Cut 3 per mat

Template B
Alternate petal to E
Cut 3 per mat

Template A
Cut 3 per mat

Vase Template D
Cut 1 per mat

Center

Message banner
for Version II

Happy Birthday

Happy Birthday

Clip ribbon ends
as shown
on the diagram.

PROJECT #15
Christmas Tree Skirt: "Katya's Angels."

45½" diameter.
Designed by the author.

Young Katya Sienkiewicz was such a cute, spunky kid. With a given name like that, it was clear her hope chest should include an Eastern European angel with braided hair, bare feet, and a swirling peasant costume. Here is her angel on a bright and easy tree skirt.

Hand Appliqué Method(s):
#2, 4, or 8 (or #3, 6, 7, 9, or 10). The model was machine appliquéd using the preparation steps for Method #5 and a satin stitch sewn using Method #5.

Appliqué Ease Level: Moderately Easy

Assembly
Iron the green skirt top into quarters, then into eighths, to mark the vertical center lines for placing each angel. Adjust the angels slightly to make room for the slit. Mark the slit with a set of two lines (½" apart, parallel) running from the inner circle, between two angels, to the outer skirt edge circle. Appliqué all the figures. Make the top/batting/backing "sandwich." The batting and backing are still untrimmed. Machine stitch the inside and outside circles of the skirt ¼" from the edge and the two sides of the slit. Trim batting and backing around the inside circle and the outside edge of the skirt. Cut the slit between the straight-stitched parallel

lines. See Project #16 for instructions on making and attaching prairie points. Attach the prairie point strips and one edge of the binding, right sides together, to the inner and outer circles. Flip binding to the back of the quilt and hand stitch. Quilt.

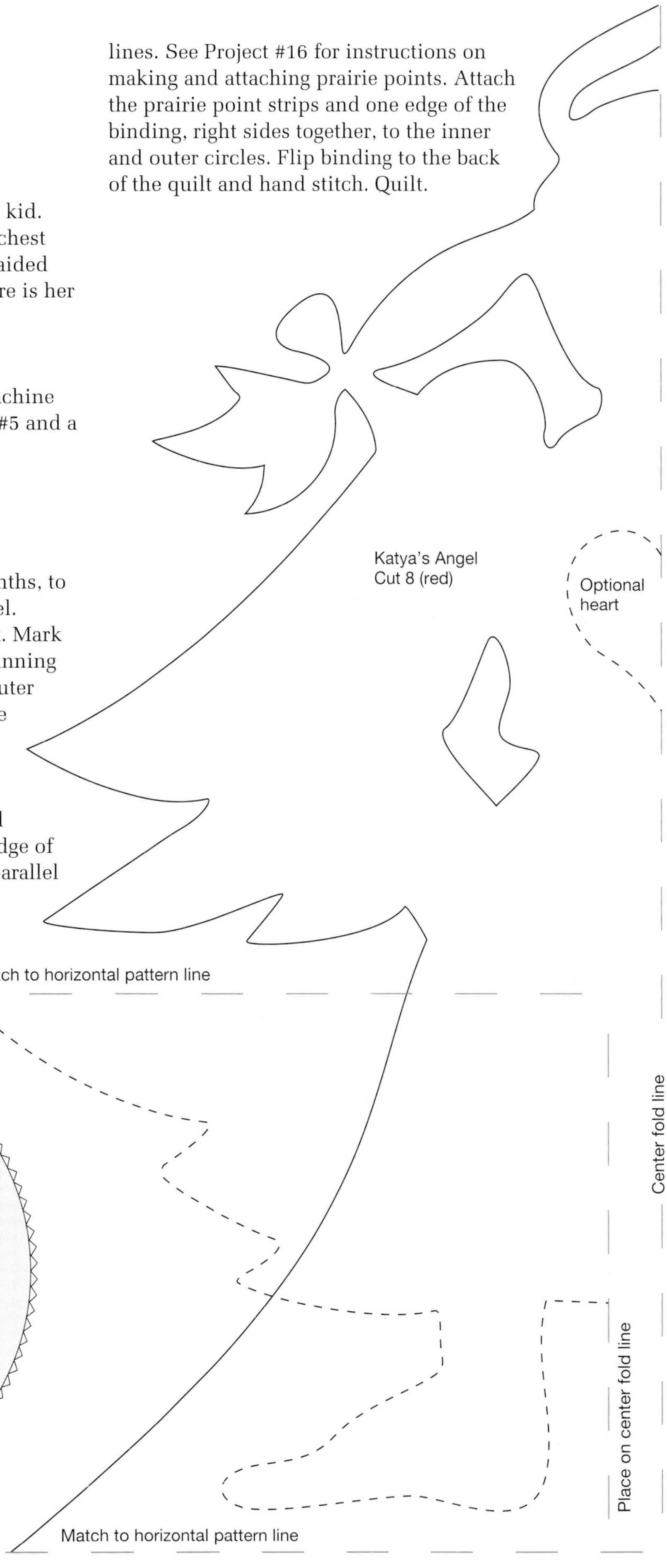

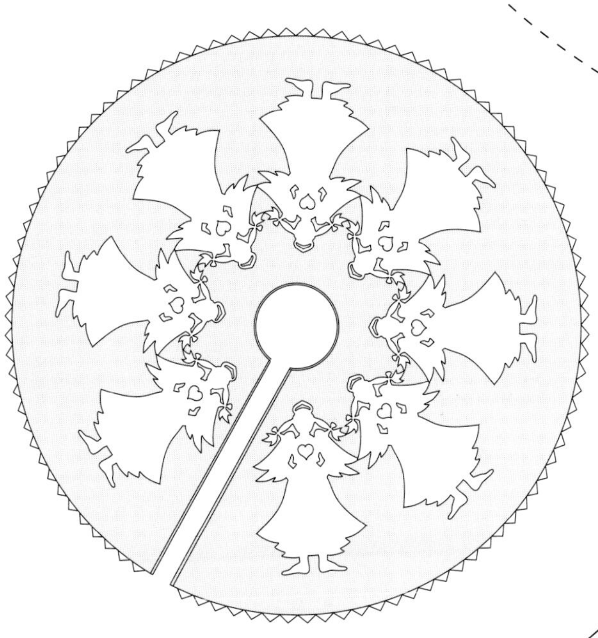

Katya's Angel
Cut 8 (red)

Optional heart

Match to horizontal pattern line

Center fold line

Place on center fold line

Match to horizontal pattern line

PROJECT #16
Small quilt: "Heart of Country."

37½" x 43½".
Designed by the author.

Hand Appliqué Method(s): #4 or #8 (or #5, 6, 7, 9, or 10).

Appliqué Ease Level: Super Easy!

Assembly

Appliqué the 14 hearts onto the border rectangles as pictured. Sew the patchwork center of the quilt. Attach the side border rectangles. Add the border corner blocks to the top and bottom borders, then sew these to the border/patchwork unit. Make prairie points (see instructions). Machine sew the strip of prairie points to the quilt top as shown. When finished, press prairie points away from the quilt top. Make a top/batting/backing sandwich; quilt, and then hem the backing to the machined seam which joins the prairie points to the top.

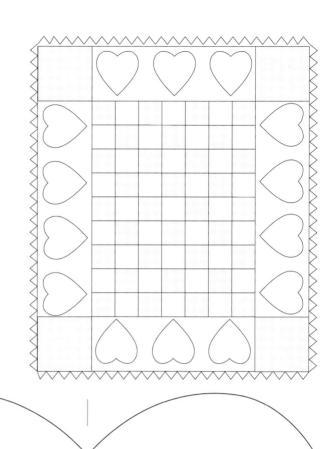

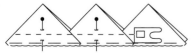

Heart Template
Cut 14

PRAIRIE POINT EDGING
To make a prairie point edging, fold each 3" square into quarters.

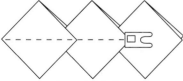

1. Nest these folded squares into each other, machine sewing through their centers as each new one is added.

2. When the strip is sewn, cut off the raw edge side of the folded squares. Pin the strip to the right side of the quilt top, raw edges together. Stitch ¼" away from the raw edges. When finished, press the prairie points away from the quilt top.

3" Square Template
Cut 32 Blue
Cut 31 White

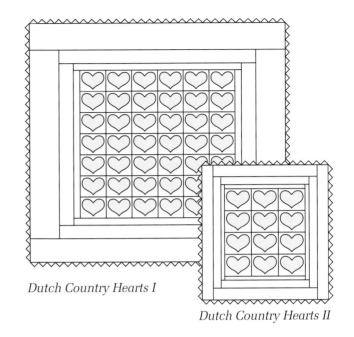

PROJECT #17
Small quilt: "Dutch Country Hearts Version I" (parent's quilt).

59½" x 56".

"Dutch Country Hearts Version II" (child's quilt).

35½" x 34¼".
Both designed by the author.

Hand Appliqué Method(s): #2, 4, 8 (or #1, 3, 5, 6, 7, 9, or 10). The model was prepared as for Method #5, but then machine appliquéd using a satin stitch.

Appliqué Ease Level: Super Easy!

Assembly for both versions
Appliqué the hearts. Set the blocks together. The easiest way to add borders is to attach the shortest ones first, proceeding from inner to outer borders. Put the prairie point edging on by machine. Make a top/batting/backing sandwich, then quilt. Trim backing and hem to machined prairie point seam.

Dutch Country Hearts I

Dutch Country Hearts II

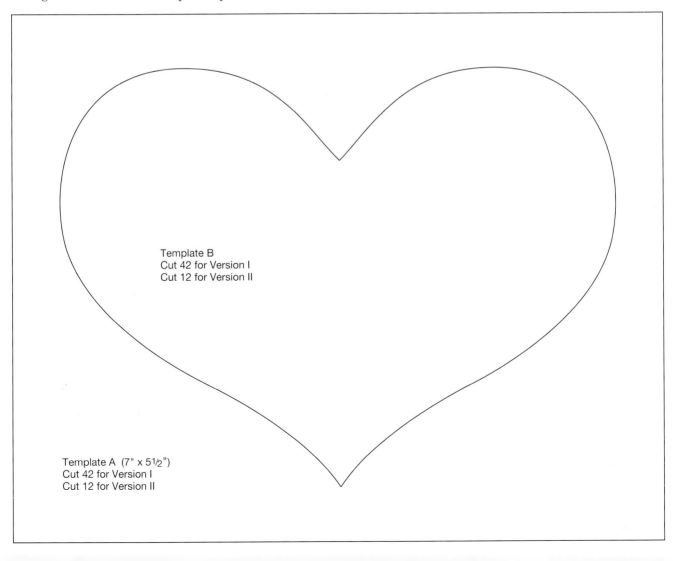

Template B
Cut 42 for Version I
Cut 12 for Version II

Template A (7" x 5½")
Cut 42 for Version I
Cut 12 for Version II

PROJECT #18
Small quilt: "Holly, Bows, and Berries."

36" x 36".
Designed by Jeannie Koch.

Hand Appliqué Method(s): #8 (or #4, 5, 6, 7, 9, or 10). For the border stems, use Method #11, taking a ⅛" seam allowance. The model was machine appliquéd, using the satin stitch and the preparation steps for Method #5. It is machine embellished and hand quilted.

Appliqué Ease Level: Easy

Assembly
Minimally mark the background fabric for blocks and borders. Embroider the stems using the stem stitch, the chain stitch, or Method #11. Then sew the leaves, and add the berries (which could be stuffed). Appliqué the blocks and borders, starting with the stems. Join the four blocks. Add the borders, mitering the corners. Make a top/batting/backing sandwich; quilt, and bind.

Horizontal center of 12" block

Vertical center of 12" block

Cut

Connect to 5-leaf
segment on top
half of block

Center of border
(stem extends down
off border)

PROJECT #19
Small quilt: "Mini-Sunbonnet Sue."

25" x 25".
Designed by Suzanne (Sue) W. Linker.

Hand Appliqué Method(s): #5 or #4 (or #1, 2, 3, 6, 7, 8, 9, or 10)

Appliqué Ease Level: Super Easy!

Assembly

Trace the pieces of Sunbonnet Sue onto the fusible web. Blanket-stitch appliqué all exposed edges. Set blocks and sashing strips together. Add border background, mitering corners. Miter corners on the blue border fabric by machine, then sew by cut-away appliqué. Make top/batting/backing sandwich; quilt, and bind.

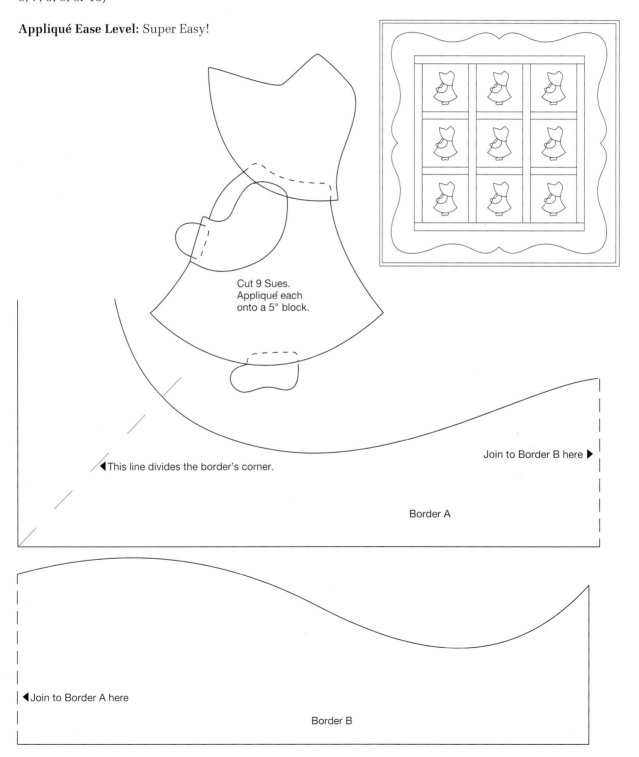

Cut 9 Sues.
Appliqué each
onto a 5" block.

◀This line divides the border's corner.

Join to Border B here ▶

Border A

◀Join to Border A here

Border B

PROJECT #20
Small quilt: "Sugar Cookies."

42" x 42".
Designed by the author.

Hand Appliqué Method(s):
Hearts: #2, 1, 4, or 8 (or #5, 6, 7, 9, or 10). This quilt could also easily be machine done by satin stitch using Method #5, or by blind hemstitch using Method #8.
Borders: Method #3, 2, or 1.

Appliqué Ease Level: The blocks are Super Easy! The border is A Challenge.

Assembly
Appliqué hearts; join blocks by rows to form a square. Join all four borders, mitering the corners. Appliqué borders. Piece the inner borders and attach to the heart center. Inset the heart center into the appliquéd feather border. Make top/batting/backing sandwich; quilt, and bind.

MACHINE APPLIQUÉ HINT:
A border like that on "Sugar Cookies" is slow and pleasant done by hand. By machine, the sewing would be quick, and, by comparison, the preparation tedious. To make it easier, try the preparation for Method #1. Since you can see through the off-white background fabric, trace the feather design right onto the wrong side of the border fabric. Straight-stitch this design through to the red appliqué fabric (right side down) pinned underneath. Trim the red back to the stitch line, then do red satin stitching on the right side of the red fabric to cover both straight-stitching and raw edge. Or use Method #2. Stack-cut two border-length feather motifs out of freezer paper at once. (For machine work, these patterns are reusable on the second two borders.) Iron a pattern to the right side of the red. Straight-stitch the appliqué seam line (to the border pinned beneath), following the edge of the freezer-paper pattern. Remove the pattern, then cut tight against the stitches to release the excess fabric. Satin stitch the presewn edge.

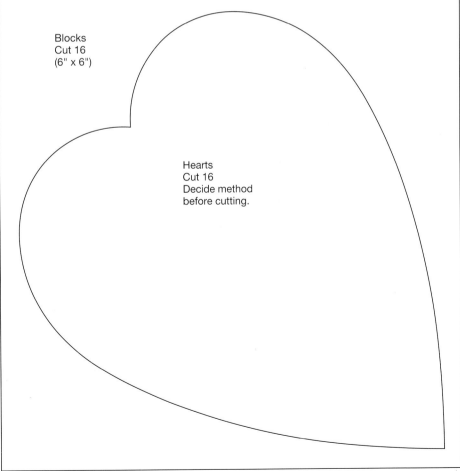

Blocks
Cut 16
(6" x 6")

Hearts
Cut 16
Decide method
before cutting.

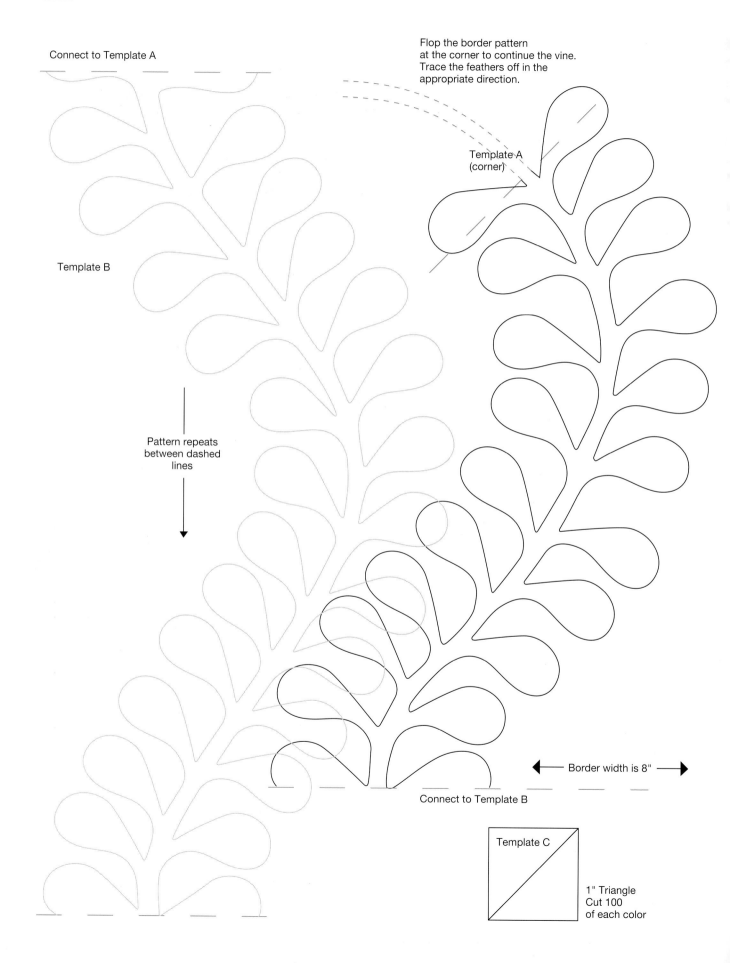

Connect to Template A

Flop the border pattern
at the corner to continue the vine.
Trace the feathers off in the
appropriate direction.

Template A
(corner)

Template B

Pattern repeats
between dashed
lines

Border width is 8"

Connect to Template B

Template C

1" Triangle
Cut 100
of each color

PROJECT #21
Small quilt: "Honey Bee Hearts."

55" x 55".
Designed by the author.

This quilt is based on the antique block pattern "Honey Bee." Its unusual color combination was also inspired by a nineteenth-century Honey Bee baby quilt.

Hand Appliqué Method(s): #4 or #8. (To blind hemstitch by machine, use Method #8; to satin stitch by machine, #5.)

Appliqué Ease Level: Super Easy!

Assembly
Piece the nine basic blocks made of 12 template G's and one template A. Then appliqué templates B, C, D, E, and F to them. Join the nine blocks together, adding the sashings and corner squares as shown. Attach top and bottom inner borders, then the side borders with the corner squares. Join the top and bottom outer borders, then the outer side borders. Make a top/batting/backing sandwich; quilt, and bind.

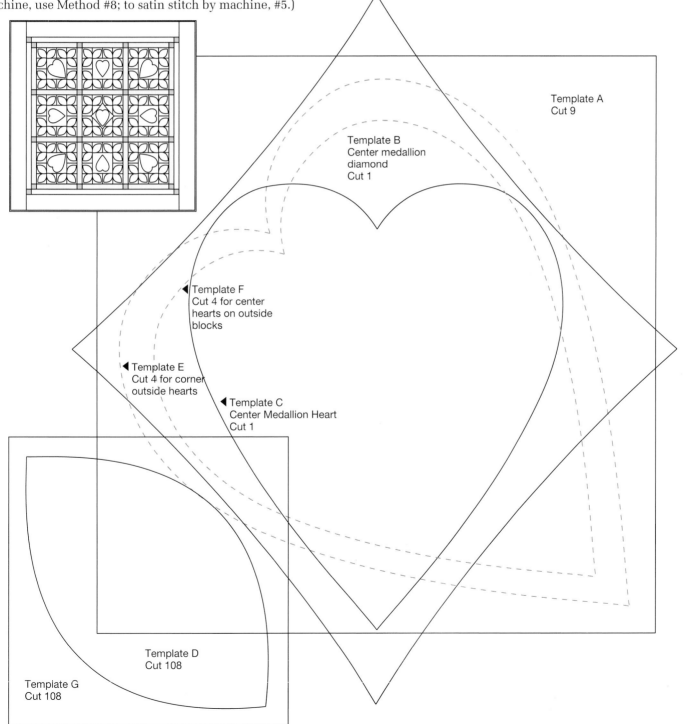

Template A
Cut 9

Template B
Center medallion
diamond
Cut 1

Template F
Cut 4 for center
hearts on outside
blocks

Template E
Cut 4 for corner
outside hearts

Template C
Center Medallion Heart
Cut 1

Template D
Cut 108

Template G
Cut 108

PROJECT #22
Small quilt: "Heartsong."

30" x 30".
Designed by Suzanne (Sue) W. Linker.

Hand Appliqué Method(s): For the quilt center: Method #8 (or #4, 5, 6, 7, 8, 9, 10) plus Method #11 for the stems. For the border, Method #4, 2, 1, or 5.

Appliqué Ease Level: Super Easy!

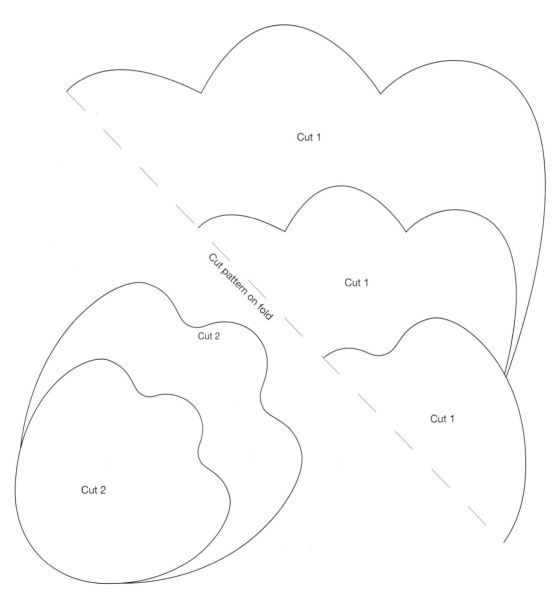

Cut 1

Cut 1

Cut pattern on fold

Cut 2

Cut 2

Cut 1

Assembly

Iron the 30½" background square diagonally into quarters, for the basic placement grid. Then minimally mark the background as discussed in Chapter 3. Appliqué the side stems first, then the center, cutting bias strips to size. Complete the central design, then the borders. Make top/batting/backing sandwich; quilt, and bind.

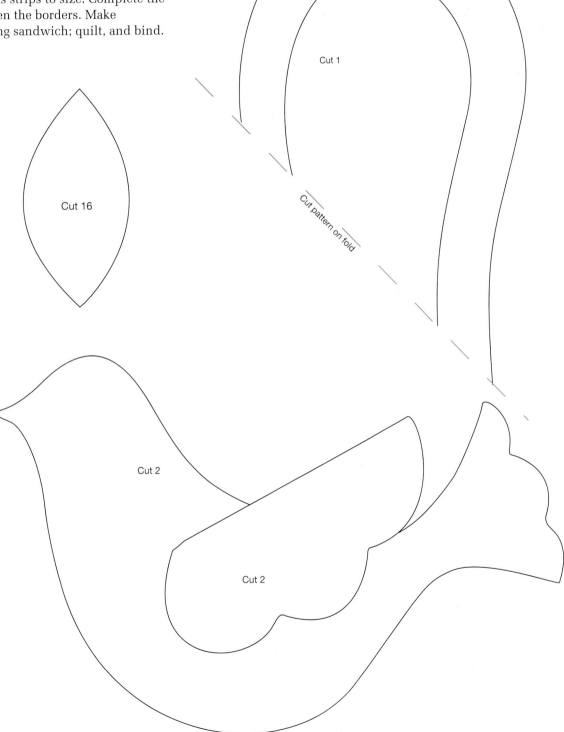

Cut 1

Cut 1

Cut pattern on fold

Cut 16

Cut 2

Cut 2

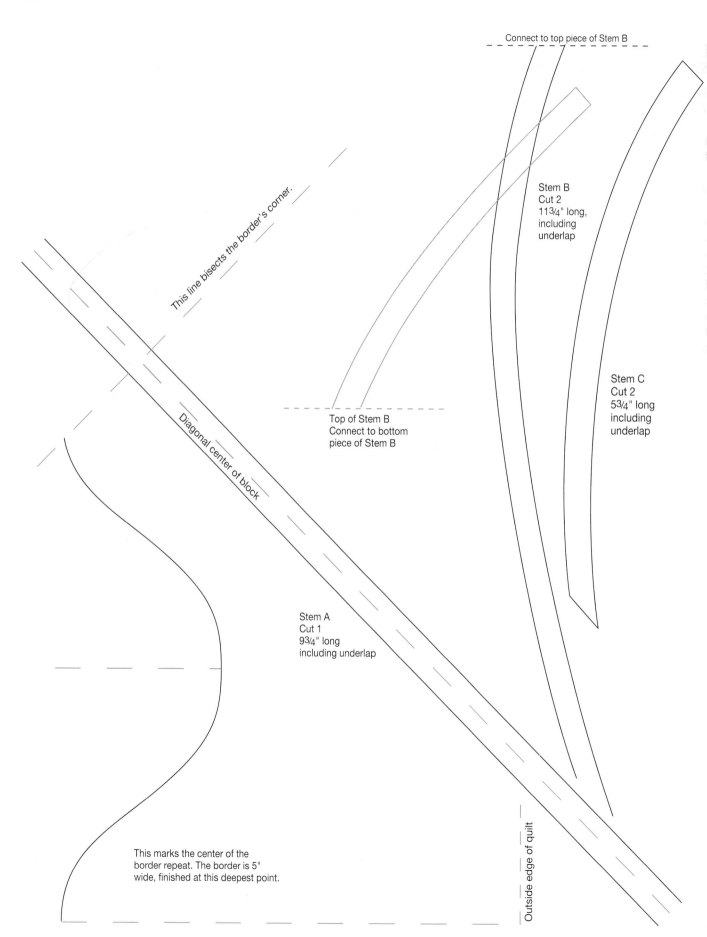

Connect to top piece of Stem B

This line bisects the border's corner.

Diagonal center of block

Stem B
Cut 2
11¾" long,
including
underlap

Stem C
Cut 2
5¾" long
including
underlap

Top of Stem B
Connect to bottom
piece of Stem B

Stem A
Cut 1
9¾" long
including underlap

Outside edge of quilt

This marks the center of the
border repeat. The border is 5"
wide, finished at this deepest point.

PROJECT #23
Small quilt: "Hearts and Crosses."

38½" x 45½".
Traditional pattern.

Hand Appliqué Method(s): #8 or #4 (or #5, 6, 7, 9, or 10).
For the heart in the hand (template B), use Method #3.

Appliqué Ease Level: Super Easy!

Assembly
Appliqué the heart blocks first, then appliqué the four corner blocks. If you reverse appliqué the miniature hearts (Method #3), do so before applying the hands to the background blocks. Sew hearts and crosses blocks together with the one-piece squares. Add the short borders to the top and bottom. Add the corner blocks to the side borders before attaching the borders to complete the quilt top. Make top/batting/backing sandwich; quilt, and bind.

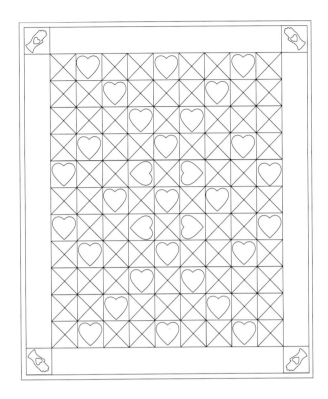

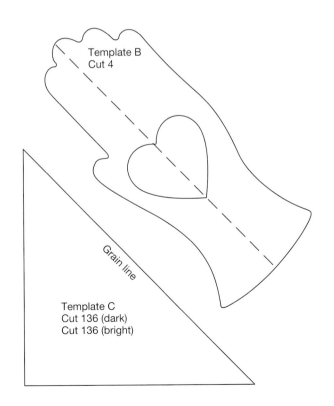

Template B
Cut 4

Grain line

Template C
Cut 136 (dark)
Cut 136 (bright)

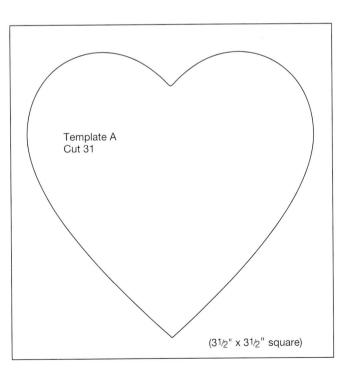

Template A
Cut 31

(3½" x 3½" square)

Project #24
Bed Quilt: "Katya's Album."

59½" x 67½".
Designed by the author.

Hand Appliqué Method(s): #5, or #2, or #1.

Appliqué Ease Level: By Method #5, Super Easy!
By Method #2 or #1, Moderately Easy.

Assembly

Inscribe the two heart centers before doing the blanket-stitch appliqué. (Have traceable calligraphed words typeset by a printer or by someone with a calligraphy-like computer font.) Add the borders in their numbered order. After border #5, add the 28 patchwork squares (made from templates C and D) and the 28 white squares. Then complete the borders. Add the prairie point edging. Make top/batting/backing sandwich; quilt, and then hem the backing to the prairie point seam. Inscribe the pieced blocks before or after they are sewn into the top.

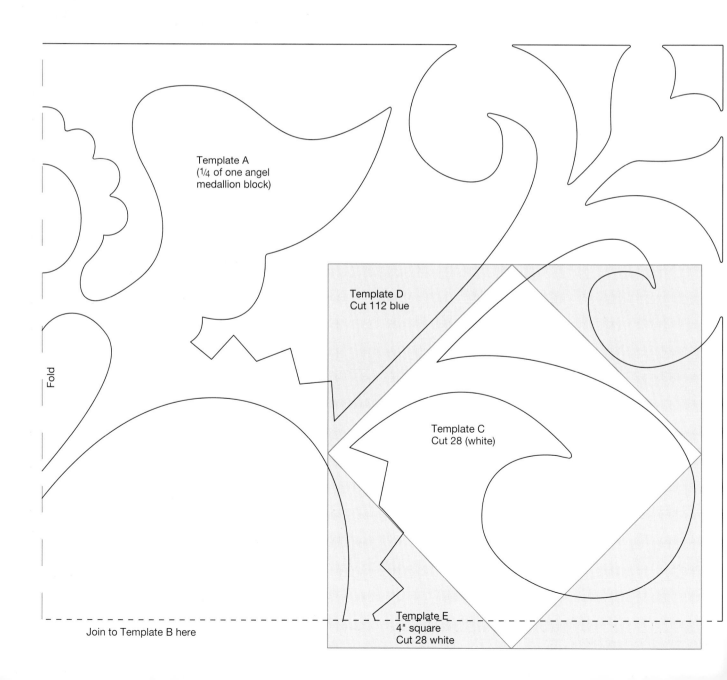

Template A
(¼ of one angel
medallion block)

Fold

Template D
Cut 112 blue

Template C
Cut 28 (white)

Template E
4" square
Cut 28 white

Join to Template B here

CENTER MEDALLION PATTERN

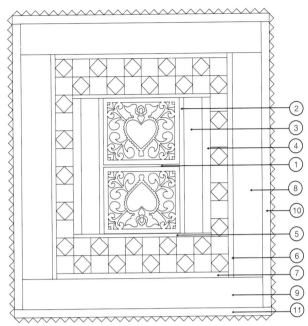

1. *Trace combined Templates A/B onto the right-hand side of a folded 15" x 18½" rectangle of fusible web. Next, trace the mirror image of this design onto the left side.*

2. *Iron this to the back of the 15" x 18½" rectangle of blue fabric. Proceed as in Method #5, making two center angel blocks. Join these two blocks with border 1. Note: This is one way to use fusible web, cutting the shape out of both the fusible and the backing at the same time.*

Join to Template A here

Template B
(¼ of one angel medallion block)

Fold

← One-half of pattern is 7¼" →

PROJECT #25
Bed quilt: "Hearts and Flowers Border Quilt."

68" x 85".
Traditional pattern.

Hand Appliqué Method(s): #2, #1, or #8 (also #5, 6, 7, or 10).

Appliqué Ease Level: Super Easy!

Assembly
Appliqué the blocks and borders. Set the three vertical rows of blocks together first, including the sashing strips between them. Join these three vertical rows of blocks together, including the four vertical sashing strips. Add the top and bottom sashing strips and borders, and then the vertical borders. Make top/batting/backing sandwich; quilt, and bind.

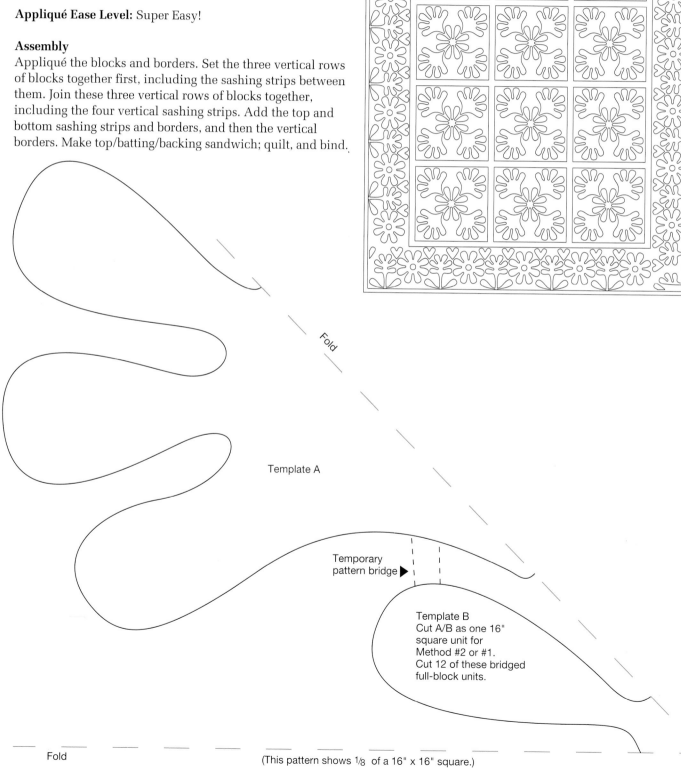

Fold

Template A

Temporary
pattern bridge ▶

Template B
Cut A/B as one 16"
square unit for
Method #2 or #1.
Cut 12 of these bridged
full-block units.

Fold

(This pattern shows ⅛ of a 16" x 16" square.)

Block pattern: *Fold a 16" square of freezer paper into quarters, then into eighths. Trace combined template A/B pattern, staple together the eight layers, and cut through all. Leave the temporary pattern bridges in place until the pattern is ironed to the right side of the blue square, then snip off. Proceed as in Method #2. For separate unit appliqué, cut 48 of template A and 12 of template B, adding seam allowance.*

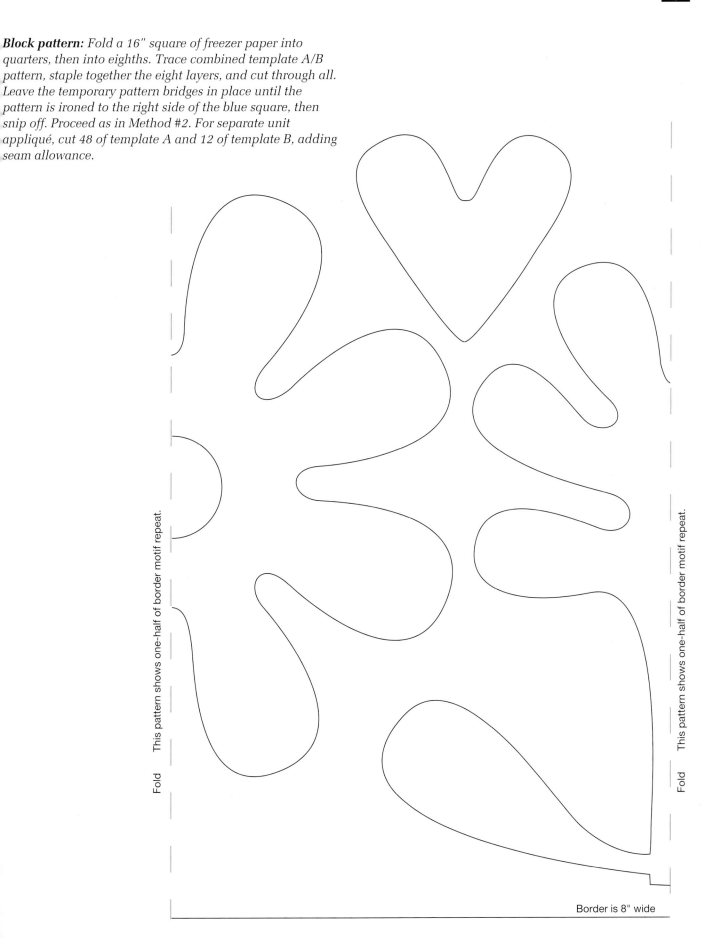

Fold   This pattern shows one-half of border motif repeat.

Fold   This pattern shows one-half of border motif repeat.

Border is 8" wide

PROJECT #26
Bed quilt: "Oak Leaves and Reel."

85" x 103".
Traditional pattern.

Hand Appliqué Method(s): #2, #1, or #8
(also #5, 6, 7, or 10).

Appliqué Ease Level: Super Easy!

Assembly
Appliqué the blocks, transferring the pattern as in Project #25. Set the four vertical rows of blocks together first, including the sashing strips between them. Join these four vertical rows of blocks together, including the three vertical sashing strips between them. Add the top and bottom borders, and the vertical borders last. Make top/batting/backing sandwich; quilt, and bind.

Fold

Template B
Mark on 6 squares

Leaf appliqué patterns
are shown as one-eighth
of a 16" x 16" finished
square.

Fold

NOTE: *When tracing a slightly more complex freezer-paper template, do not allow the pattern to "grow" by tracing outside its drawn lines. When cutting it out, cut off the pencil lines. If pencil lines show, particularly at inward points, the paper template is stealing some of the fabric space needed for seam allowances. On a timesaving note, remember that symmetrical patterns can always be traced by half, pinned or stapled (so that the layers don't shift), and cut double.*

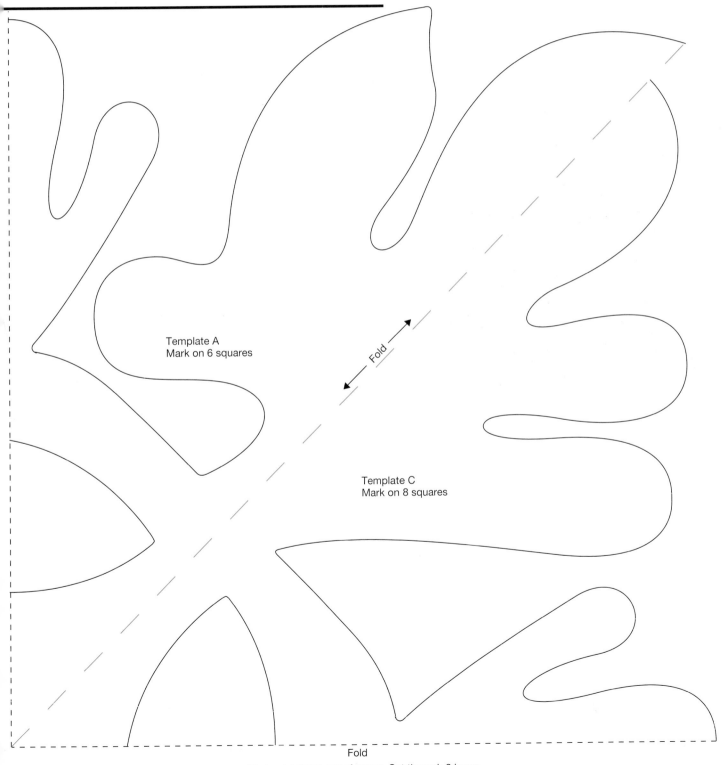

Template A
Mark on 6 squares

Fold

Template C
Mark on 8 squares

Fold
First cut pattern out of paper. Cut through 8 layers.

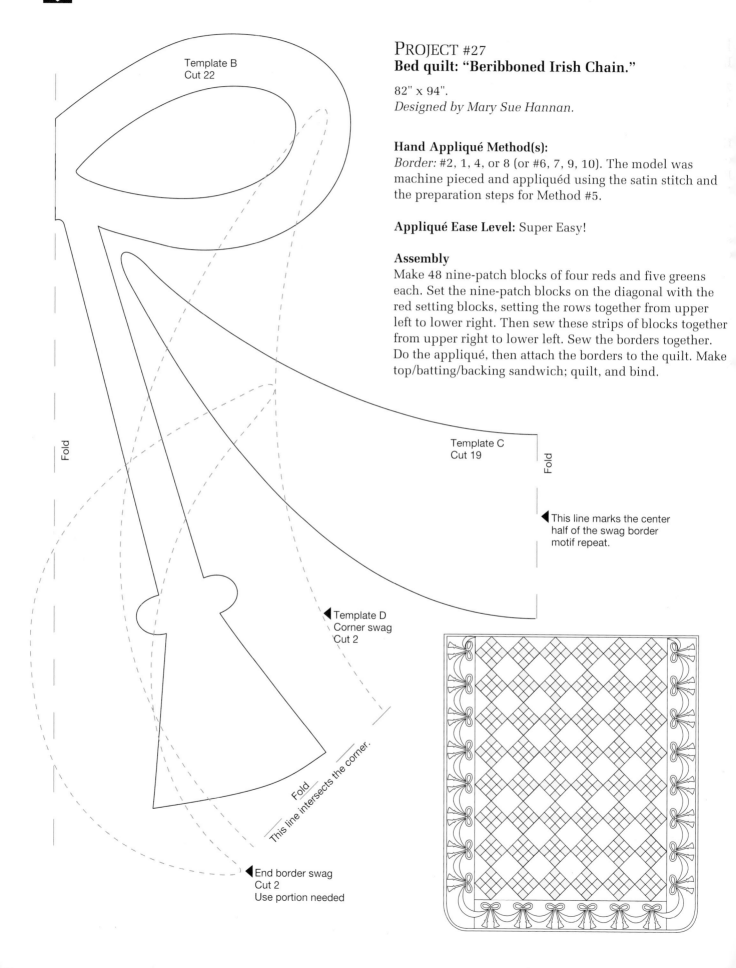

Template B
Cut 22

Fold

PROJECT #27
Bed quilt: "Beribboned Irish Chain."

82" x 94".
Designed by Mary Sue Hannan.

Hand Appliqué Method(s):
Border: #2, 1, 4, or 8 (or #6, 7, 9, 10). The model was machine pieced and appliquéd using the satin stitch and the preparation steps for Method #5.

Appliqué Ease Level: Super Easy!

Assembly
Make 48 nine-patch blocks of four reds and five greens each. Set the nine-patch blocks on the diagonal with the red setting blocks, setting the rows together from upper left to lower right. Then sew these strips of blocks together from upper right to lower left. Sew the borders together. Do the appliqué, then attach the borders to the quilt. Make top/batting/backing sandwich; quilt, and bind.

Template C
Cut 19

Fold

◀ This line marks the center half of the swag border motif repeat.

◀ Template D
Corner swag
Cut 2

Fold
This line intersects the corner.

◀ End border swag
Cut 2
Use portion needed

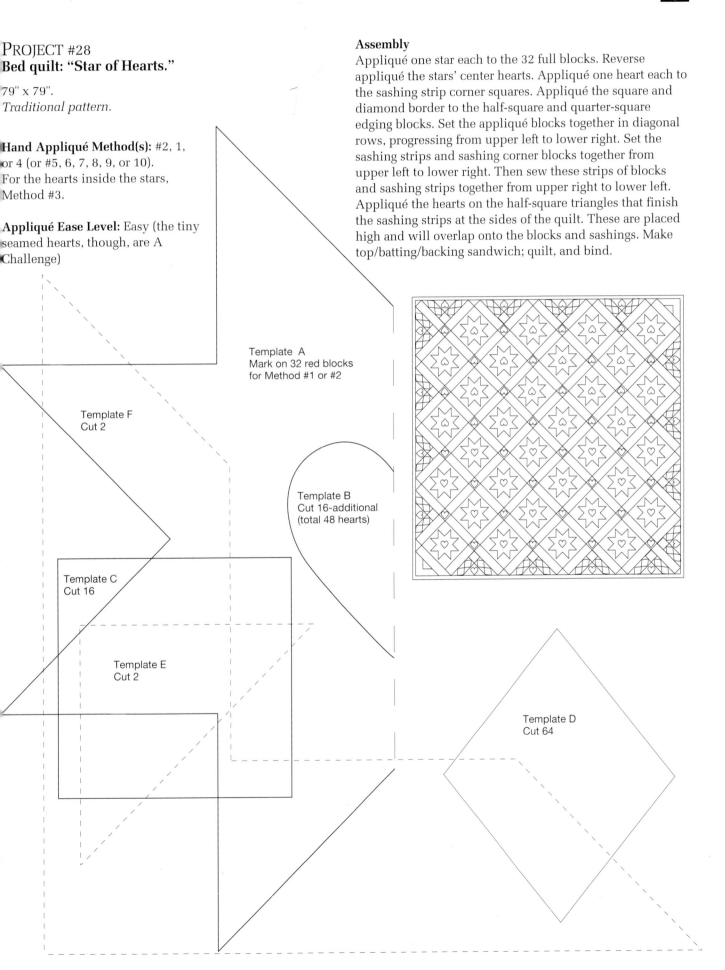

PROJECT #28
Bed quilt: "Star of Hearts."

79" x 79".
Traditional pattern.

Hand Appliqué Method(s): #2, 1, or 4 (or #5, 6, 7, 8, 9, or 10). For the hearts inside the stars, Method #3.

Appliqué Ease Level: Easy (the tiny seamed hearts, though, are A Challenge)

Assembly

Appliqué one star each to the 32 full blocks. Reverse appliqué the stars' center hearts. Appliqué one heart each to the sashing strip corner squares. Appliqué the square and diamond border to the half-square and quarter-square edging blocks. Set the appliqué blocks together in diagonal rows, progressing from upper left to lower right. Set the sashing strips and sashing corner blocks together from upper left to lower right. Then sew these strips of blocks and sashing strips together from upper right to lower left. Appliqué the hearts on the half-square triangles that finish the sashing strips at the sides of the quilt. These are placed high and will overlap onto the blocks and sashings. Make top/batting/backing sandwich; quilt, and bind.

Template A
Mark on 32 red blocks
for Method #1 or #2

Template F
Cut 2

Template B
Cut 16-additional
(total 48 hearts)

Template C
Cut 16

Template E
Cut 2

Template D
Cut 64

Project #29
Bed quilt: "Twining Blooms and Baskets."

67" x 79¾".
Pattern designed by the author.

Hand Appliqué Method(s): #2 for basket blocks and vine, Method #11 for border stripes, and Method #4 for flowers.

Appliqué Ease Level:
Baskets and border stripes: Easy! The border rates Moderately Easy because of the layered flowers. (To simplify, make the bell flower two layers instead of three by leaving out template #10.)

Assembly
Appliqué the baskets. Inscribe centers if this is an Album Quilt. Appliqué the borders. Sew the patchwork center of the quilt by first attaching blocks to form diagonal rows from upper left to lower right. Then sew these rows to each other from right to left. Attach the borders clockwise.

Border Detail

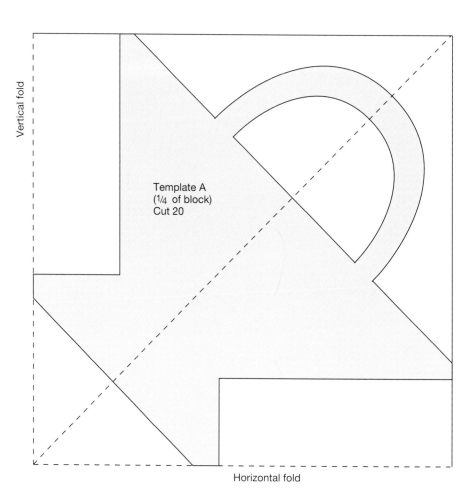

Vertical fold

Template A
(¼ of block)
Cut 20

Horizontal fold

Mirror these two stripes on the inside of the border. (These will be border stripes #3 and #4.)

Border 8"

ELLY HAMILTON SIENKIEWICZ has been making quilts for seventeen years and writing about them for ten. This is her fifth book about appliqué. A history teacher by training, she reflects the influence of her artist mother and her West Virginia quiltmaking relatives, Cousin Wilma Clarice Hamilton Tallman and Great Aunt Shirley Atha Freeland Hamilton Landis, who taught her the craft. Inherently a teacher (like her father and grandmother before her), Elly shares her enthusiasm, creativity, and technical knowledge in *Appliqué 12 Easy Ways!* A popular instructor, she teaches and lectures on quiltmaking around the country and around the world. Her work has been widely published and exhibited both here and abroad. Elly believes that even a beginner can have great success with hand appliqué and has written this book to prove it. She and her husband Stan live in Washington, D.C., with their children, Donald, Alex, and Katya.

If you liked *Appliqué 12 Easy Ways!*, here are more in-depth Elly Sienkiewicz books on appliqué, published by C&T Publishing, Inc.:

• *Baltimore Beauties and Beyond, Studies in Classic Album Quilt Appliqué, Volume I,* (24 appliqué blocks from simple to complex, with techniques, including additional dimensional flowers)

• *The Best of Baltimore Beauties* (95 appliqué blocks from simple to complex compiled from Elly's popular *Baltimore Beauties and Beyond Series,* including 4 new patterns)

• *Fancy Appliqué: 12 Lessons to Enhance Your Skills* (12 new lessons and 39 full-size patterns)

Other Fine Books From C&T Publishing:

• *The Art of Classic Quiltmaking,* Harriet Hargrave and Sharyn Craig
• *At Home with Patrick Lose: Colorful Quilted Projects,* Patrick Lose
• *Color From the Heart: Seven Great Ways to Make Quilts with Colors You Love,* Gai Perry
• *Curves in Motion: Quilt Designs & Techniques,* Judy B. Dales
• *Exploring Machine Trapunto: New Dimensions,* Hari Walner
• *Fabric Shopping with Alex Anderson, Seven Project to Help You: Make, Successful Choices, Build Your Confidence, Add to Your Fabric Stash,* Alex Anderson
• *Faces & Places: Images in Appliqué,* Charlotte Warr Andersen
• *Fantastic Fabric Folding: Innovative Quilting Projects,* Rebecca Wat
• *Focus on Features: Life-like Portrayals in Appliqué,* Charlotte Warr Andersen
• *Freddy's House: Brilliant Color in Quilts,* Freddy Moran
• *Hand Quilting with Alex Anderson: Six Projects for Hand Quilters,* Alex Anderson
• *Jacobean Rhapsodies: Composing with 28 Appliqué Designs,* Patricia B. Campbell and Mimi Ayars
• *Mastering Quilt Marking: Marking Tools & Techniques, Choosing Stencils, Matching Borders & Corners,* Pepper Cory
• *The Photo Transfer Handbook: Snap It, Print It, Stitch It!,* Jean Ray Laury
• *Pieced Roman Shades: Turn Your Favorite Quilt Patterns into Window Hangings,* Terrell Sundermann
• *Piecing: Expanding the Basics,* Ruth B. McDowell
• *Quilts from Europe, Projects and Inspiration,* Gül Laporte
• *Rotary Cutting with Alex Anderson: Tips, Techniques, and Projects,* Alex Anderson
• *Rx for Quilters: Stitcher-Friendly Advice for Every Body,* Susan Delaney Mech, M.D.
• *Skydyes: A Visual Guide to Fabric Painting,* Mickey Lawler
• *Special Delivery Quilts,* Patrick Lose
• *Start Quilting with Alex Anderson: Six Projects for First-Time Quilters,* Alex Anderson
• *Through the Garden Gate: Quilters and Their Gardens,* Jean and Valori Wells
• *Travels with Peaky and Spike: Doreen Speckmann's Quilting Adventures,* Doreen Speckmann
• *Wild Birds: Designs for Appliqué & Quilting,* Carol Armstrong
• *Wildflowers: Designs for Appliqué & Quilting,* Carol Armstrong
• *Women of Taste: A Collaboration Celebrating Quilt Artists and Chefs,* Girls, Inc.

For more information write for a free catalog:
C&T Publishing, Inc.
P.O. Box 1456
Lafayette, CA 94549
e-mail: ctinfo@ctpub.com
www.ctpub.com
(800) 284-1114

For quilting supplies:
Cotton Patch Mail Order
3405 Hall Lane, Dept. CTB
Lafayette, CA 94549
e-mail: quiltusa@yahoo.com
www.quiltusa.com
(800) 835-4418
(925) 283-7883